NEXT
PROPHECIES

DECLINE OF ISLAM
EZEKIEL 38
MYSTERY BABYLON
THE ANTICHRIST

BILL SALUS
Author of The NOW Prophecies

The Next Prophecies
First printing October 2018

Prophecy Depot Publishing
Customer Service: 714-376-5487
P.O. Box 5612

La Quinta, CA 92248

ISBN – 978-0-692-17617-7

Interior and cover by Mark Conn

Printed in the United States of America

Acknowledgements

Heartfelt thanks to my wife, children, grandchildren and friends who inspired me to write this book. A further debt of gratitude is extended to Bob and Lynette Holmes, Brad Myers, Ladd Holton, the Gaskin's, Bill and Beverly Williams, Ned and Karol Bankston, Scott and Deborah Bueling, Mark Conn, our Prophecy Depot Ministry Partners and all those who in one way or another, through prayer, encouragement, support, research, or otherwise, genuinely blessed this book.

Contents

Chapter 1
Introducing the NOW, NEXT and LAST Prophecies 7

Chapter 2
The Next Prophecies of Ezekiel 38-39 13

Chapter 3
Introduction to the Post-Rapture /Pre-Tribulation Gap Period 33

Chapter 4
What Will the World Look Like Shortly After the Rapture?.. 39

Chapter 5
The Church is in Heaven Before the Antichrist is Revealed
on Earth.. 43

Chapter 6
Introducing the Antichrist 49

Chapter 7
The Two Parties of the False Covenant 59

Chapter 8
The Traditional View of the Seal Judgments of Revelation 6.. 63

Chapter 9
The Alternative View of the Seal Judgments of Revelation 6.. 77

Chapter 10
Do Death and Hades Represent the Harlot World Religion? . 87

Chapter 11
Is Islam the Harlot World Religion?................... 107

Chapter 12
Death and Hades Kill the Fifth Seal Saints? 117

Chapter 13
The Two Killing Crusades that Martyr Christians
After the Rapture 121

Chapter 14
The Three Periods of Post Rapture Christian Martyrdom . . . 127

Chapter 15
The Sixth Seal Contains the Wrath of the Lamb 135

Chapter 16
Why is the Catholic Church Cast into the Great Tribulation? 139

Chapter 17
Does Salvation Come Through the Roman Catholic Church? 151

Chapter 18
The False Covenant of Death in Agreement
with Sheol 161

Chapter 19
What is the True Content of the False Covenant? 167

Chapter 20
The Two Deadly Phases of the Overflowing Scourge. 173

Chapter 21
The Two Witnesses 177

Chapter 22
The Two Judgments of End Times Babylon 187

Chapter 23
The Mecca – Mystery Babylon Connection and Problems . . 195

Chapter 24
Why Jerusalem, New York City and Literal Babylon are not
Mystery Babylon 201

Appendices
1 The Revised Apocalyptic Timeline 209
2 The Seven Letters to the Churches 214
3 IRAN is in Ezekiel 38, but why NOT their PROXIES? . 218
4 The Sinner's Salvation Prayer 225

Endnotes 236

Introducing the NOW, NEXT and LAST Prophecies

When it comes to understanding the remaining unfulfilled Bible prophecies, one of the most important factors to consider is their timing. It is crucial to know when the predicted events provided within the epic prophetic event will happen!

There are three easy to understand categories of coming biblical prophecies. They are the;

1. NOW Prophecies,
2. NEXT Prophecies,
3. LAST Prophecies

ulfilled ancient biblical
ent, which means they
s have either minor or no
em from happening.

rophecy about a forthcoming
Prophecies dealt with seven years
wed up by seven years of ensuing
Jeremiah warned about seventy years
the corresponding Jewish dispersion
ears.

o.
fro

In these instances, it was the NOW Prophecies that were of the utmost benefit to the affected populations within their respective times. These timely predictions enabled the peoples of those times to prepare for the powerful events that directly affected them!

This present generation has several powerful NOW Prophecies racing towards their fulfillment. These predictions are the subject of the first book in this end time's non-fiction series called, "*The Now Prophecies*." The NOW Prophecies include, but are not limited to, the following globally impacting events. They are the:

1. Disaster in Iran – (Jeremiah 49:34-39),
2. Destruction of Damascus – (Isaiah 17, Jer. 49:23-27),
3. Final Arab-Israeli War- (Psalm 83),
4. Toppling of Jordan – (Jer. 49:1-6, Zephaniah 2:8-10, Ezekiel 25:14),
5. Terrorization of Egypt – (Isaiah 19:1-18),
6. Emergence of the exceedingly great Israeli army – (Ezekiel 37:10, 25:14, Obadiah 1:18),
7. Expansion of Israel – (Obadiah 1:19-20, Jer. 49:2, Zephaniah 2:9, Isaiah 19:18),
8. Vanishing of the Christians – (1 Corinthians 15:51-52, 1 Thessalonians 4:15-18),
9. Emergence of a greater, safer and wealthier Israel – (Ezekiel 38:8-13),
10. Decline of America – (Ezekiel 38:13), (*USA could be the young lions of Tarshish*).

The NEXT Prophecies

The NEXT Prophecies are those that follow the fulfillment of the above NOW Prophecies. The Now Prophecies provides the necessary nexus of events that pave the path for the execution of the coming Next Prophecies. Although the Next Prophecies are rapidly racing toward fulfillment, they require the completion of the Now's for their stage to become appropriately set.

What distinguishes the Now Prophecies from the Next Prophecies, is that the Next Prophecies have at least one or more significant preconditions prohibiting their final fulfillment. Although these Next Prophecies appear to be presently stage setting, their completion is being prevented by some other epic prophetic event, or series of events.

It is important to be aware of both the Now and Next Prophecies because they are all converging presently. The present generation could be confronted with a plethora of overpowering prophetic events. These ancient prophecies were not meant to remain on their parchments indefinitely. In their due course of time they are scheduled to roll off their parchments and pound down on the pavement packing a powerful universal punch. I suggest that they will have a worldwide effect because all end times Bible prophecies appear to be globally impacting.

The LAST Prophecies

The LAST Prophecies still have significant preconditions preventing them from finding fulfillment. They will find fulfillment relatively soon, but the LAST's must wait in line behind the NOW's and NEXT's for their turn on the prophetic timeline.

Summary

An instructor at a seminary was teaching about Bible prophecy one day and he prefaced his talk by asking the students, "*What are the two main problems confronting Christians today when it comes to understanding biblical prophecy?*"

To his chagrin, he noticed that not one hand was raised in response to his question. So, the teacher glanced across his class and noticed that one student was demonstrating a disinterest in the topic by texting on his phone. He singled the individual out and asked him to answer the question, "*Young man can you tell me; What are the two main problems confronting Christians today when it comes to understanding biblical prophecy?*"

Evidencing his blatant disregard for Bible prophecy, the student stood up, pounded his hand down on his desk in frustration and blurted out; "I DON'T KNOW *and* I DON'T CARE!

"EXACTLY," the professor responded. "*That's the correct answer I was looking for!*"

•   •   •

There are hundreds of biblically predicted details, which are described in several thousand verses, that remain unfulfilled. Many Bible prophecy experts believe that these looming epic prophetic events are converging and destined to manifest in the very near future.

Due to their enormity, they won't all happen at the same time, rather they will be strategically ordered in an understandable sequence over a short time span. Unfortunately, like our student in the story above, many Christians are unfamiliar with these epic events and don't take time to educate themselves about them. In many cases they don't know because they don't care.

When it comes to addressing the Now, Next and Last Prophecies, the logical questions are:

1. What are the remaining unfulfilled prophecies?
2. How will they sequence out?
3. When will they find fulfillment?
4. Why should I care?
5. How will they affect me and my family?
6. How much time do I have to prepare for these prophecies?

The answers to these questions are provided in this book series. They are outlined in the logical categorical orders of *NOW, NEXT* and *LAST.* These books are purposely designed to explain to the reader why they should care and how they should prepare.

In a general overview, some or all of the Now Prophecies identified above could occur during the Church Age. However, the Rapture, which concludes the Church Age, could happen before any of the other Now Prophecies happen. If so, those unfulfilled Now Prophecies will likely find their completion within the prophetic gap period that exists between the Rapture and the seven-year Tribulation Period, (Trib-period). This period is also referred to as "Daniel's Seventieth Week."

The prophetic time-gap is a central theme of this book. Some of the Next Prophecies should find fulfillment within this gap interval. The Last Prophecies are mostly concerning the prophecies that occur during the Trib-period.

2

The Next Prophecies of Ezekiel 38-39

This chapter provides an overview of the epic end times events described in Ezekiel 38 and 39 and explains why it is a Next, rather than a Now Prophecy. It also explores why the event probably occurs prior to the seven-year Tribulation Period. Other topics covered are:

- What are the conditions in Israel before the Gog of Magog invasion? (Ezekiel 38:1-13).

- What are the conditions in Israel during the invasion? (Ezekiel 38:14-39:8).

- What are the conditions in Israel in the aftermath? (Ezekiel 39:9-21).

Most contemporary commentaries on Ezekiel 38 approach the prophecy as if it could happen while Israel is dwelling in its present geographic location, socio-economic status and geo-political condition. However, that is not the perspective presented in this chapter. The fulfillment of the NOW Prophecies mentioned in chapter one should dramatically change Israel's future complexion. The coming Israel described in Ezekiel 38:8-13 appears to be greater in size, safer in national security and more economically prosperous than the Israel of today, making it a NEXT Prophecy.

Currently, Israel is slightly over 8,000 square miles, which is about the size of New Jersey. It is surrounded by Arab states and terrorist populations that don't recognize Israel's right to exist as the Jewish State. If you believe that Ezekiel 38 finds fulfillment while Israel exists in its current geo-political condition, then how would you answer the following questions?

1. *Why does Russia (Magog) need such a big coalition to invade today's tiny little Israel?* The general consensus among many of today's Bible prophecy teachers is that the list of the Ezekiel 38 invaders includes Russia , Turkey, Iran, Libya, Ethiopia, Sudan, Somalia, Morocco, Tunisia, and perhaps a few others. Russia, Turkey, Iran, Tunisia and Libya, not including the other invaders, have populations that currently total over 300 million. When you compare this to Israel's estimated Jewish population of about 6.5 million, it seems a bit like overkill. Additionally, the Russian army is ranked #2, the Turkish army is ranked #9 and Iranian army is ranked #13 among world armies. In comparison, Israel is presently ranked #16.[1] *(For a visual layout of the Ezekiel 38 countries refer to the Outer Ring of nations map image in the chapter entitled, Is Islam the Harlot World Religion).*

2. *Why doesn't Ezekiel include the Arab states that share common borders with Israel among the Gog of Magog invaders?* After all, these Arabs are the notorious enemies of Israel in the past and still today, but none of the invaders in Ezekiel 38 have ever been historic enemies of Israel. (Excluding perhaps Persia at the time of Esther around 486-468 BC). Ezekiel is familiar with these Arab populations, he lists them by their historic names at least 89 times in his 48 chapters, but seemingly intentionally omits them among the lineup of the Ezekiel invaders.

3. *Is Israel dwelling securely without walls, bars or gates as per Ezekiel 38:11?* Israel has approximately a 400-mile-long wall that runs through much of Israel. In fact, it can be argued that Israel is the most fenced in and fortified

country in the world. Additionally, Israel has multiple security checkpoints located throughout the country. Also, some of the Jewish settlements inside of Israel have fences around them. Below are a few telling headlines about Israel's security walls.

Israel completes Lebanon border wall around Metulla – 6/12/2012, Times of Israel.

Israel resumes construction of wall along Lebanon border – 4/10/2018, Middle East Monitor.

Israel starts massive fence on southern border with Jordan – 1/20/2016, Times of Israel.

Israel starts building sea barrier to defend against Gaza attacks – 5/27/2018, Times of Israel.

Israel unveils plans for 40-mile underground wall around Gaza – 1/18/2018, The Telegraph.

Palestinian protesters breach Israel-Gaza border fence; 3 killed, hundreds injured in clashes – 4/27/2018, Los Angeles Times.

Observe that most of the headline dates above are relatively recent. This suggests that Israel is not presently dwelling securely. Otherwise, they would not need to construct new walls, nor extend existing walls.

4. *Does Israel possess the enormous amount of booty and plunder that the Magog invaders desire as per Ezekiel 38:12-13?* Israel has discovered large sources of natural gas, but Russia has no shortage of gas. Some sources place Russia as the #2 supplier in the world of natural gas. Also, Russia is among the top three oil exporting countries in the world.

These are just a few questions, which upon a close examination, seems to suggest that the Gog of Magog invaders won't coalesce to invade today's Israel. However, if some of the NOW Prophecies precede Ezekiel 38, then these same four questions could be answered in this manner;

1. *Why does Russia (Magog) need such a big coalition to invade today's tiny little Israel?*

   Russia needs to formulate a big coalition to invade Israel because;

   a. The Israeli Defense Forces (IDF) have become an exceedingly great army in fulfillment of Ezekiel 37:10, 25:14, Obadiah 1:18, Zechariah 12:4-6, Isaiah 11:12-14 and elsewhere.

   b. The IDF accomplished this by decisively defeating the Arabs in Psalm 83, destroying Damascus in Isaiah 17:1, 9, 14 and toppling Jordan in Jeremiah 49:2 and Zephaniah 2:8-9.

   c. Furthermore, the tiny Jewish state of 2018 has become a significantly larger Israel. This resulted from annexing the formerly occupied Arab lands identified in Obadiah 1:19-20, Zephaniah 2:9, Isaiah 19:18 and Jeremiah 49:2.

2. *Why doesn't Ezekiel include the Arab states that share common borders with Israel among the Gog of Magog invaders?*

   The Arab states are already defeated by the IDF in fulfillment of the Psalm 83 war.

3. *Is Israel dwelling securely without walls, bars or gates as per Ezekiel 38:11?*

a. Israel is dwelling securely because the IDF has defeated their neighboring enemies. As a result, they have militarily, rather than politically, achieved the national security that they had desperately longed for since becoming a nation in 1948.

b. Another possible reason is that they have torn down the partition wall and removed all security checkpoints within the country, after the defeat of their enemies in Psalms 83. Some of these security fences are eyesores on Israel's landscape. When they are no longer essential for Israel's security, they will likely be removed.

4. *Does Israel possess the enormous amount of booty and plunder that the Magog invaders desire as per Ezekiel 38:12-13?*

Not only has Israel become safer and larger as answered in the three prior questions, but they have also become wealthier. This characteristic is elaborated upon below.

What are the conditions in Israel before the Gog of Magog invasion?

Ezekiel 38:8-13, are the telling verses that describe what Israel looks like geo-politically prior to the Gog of Magog invasion.

In a summary, Ezekiel 38:8-13 informs that at the time of the Gog of Magog invasion that Israel will be:

1. Regathered from the nations,
2. In the "Latter Years,"
3. Brought back from the "Sword" (of persecution),
4. "Israel," which had "long been desolate,"
5. Dwell in the "midst," or center, of the Promised Land.

These four conditions have either been met, or are currently being met depending on what exactly Ezekiel meant by the "midst" of the land. Technically the midst of the Promised Land would today include the West Bank, which is mostly under Palestinian control, and perhaps the country of Jordan. Israel is not yet in control of these areas. However, the conditions #6 to #9 below have not been fulfilled yet.

6. Israel must be a "peaceful people" that are "dwelling securely."
7. The Jewish state must exist without "walls, bars nor gates."
8. The country must possess great wealth comprised of "gold and silver." and have "acquired livestock and goods."
9. Israel must be a very wealthy country possessing "great plunder and booty," because that is what the Ezekiel invaders are coming after.

Presently, Israel IS NOT dwelling without "walls, bars nor gates." Inside the country exists a partition wall that is over 400 miles long, which at some points is 20 feet tall and filled with concrete. This wall serves to separate Palestinian terror out from Israel proper. There are also security checkpoints at various places inside of Israel.

Moreover, the Jewish state IS NOT "dwelling securely" presently. They are surrounded by Arab countries and terrorist populations that don't enable them to dwell safely. Ezekiel tells us ten chapters earlier in Ezekiel 28, what will have to happen for Israel to dwell securely.

> "And there shall no longer be a pricking brier or a painful thorn for the house of Israel from among all who are around them, who despise them. Then they shall know that I am the Lord God." 'Thus says the Lord God: "When I have gathered the house of Israel from the peoples among whom they are scattered, and am hallowed in them in the sight of the Gentiles, then they will dwell in

their own land which I gave to My servant Jacob. And they WILL DWELL SAFELY there, build houses, and plant vineyards; yes, they WILL DWELL SECURELY, WHEN I EXECUTE JUDGMENTS ON ALL THOSE AROUND THEM WHO DESPISE THEM. Then they shall know that I am the Lord their God.""" (Ezekiel 28:14-16; emphasis added)

These verses tell us that Israel will dwell securely when their surrounding Arab neighbors who despise the Jewish state have judgments executed upon them. Until Israel dwells securely Ezekiel 38 will continue to be a NEXT Prophecy. Many of these judgments that Ezekiel 28 predicts must happen are seemingly part of the NOW Prophecies listed in chapter one.

Presuming some or all of the NOW Prophecies have occurred; then Israel will be reshaping itself in response to the ten NOW prophetic scenarios presented in chapter one. The Jewish state should be understandably *larger, safer* and *wealthier*.

Recapping some of these Now Prophecies, they are, The disaster in Iran, destruction of Damascus, final Arab-Israeli war, toppling of Jordan, terrorization of Egypt, emergence of the exceedingly great Israeli army and the territorial expansion of Israel.

This *greater, safer* and *wealthier* Israel should be conducive to an influx of more Jewish Aliyah, (Jewish migration into Israel). Jews have been making Aliyah into Israel continuously for over a century and this process will likely increase once Israel is freed from the torment of Arab terror. The threat of terror should greatly diminish after Israel defeats its Arab foes in Psalm 83 and its related peripheral prophecies already mentioned in this chapter.

Some Jews living outside of Israel are presently driven to make Aliyah to avoid present or perceived future persecution in their present homelands. However, when Israel is *larger* and *safer*, Jews can make Aliyah, not only to escape mounting international Anti-Semitism, but also to participate in the expansion of Israel into a *wealthier* nation. The skills and wealth they bring with them could become a contributing factor that leads to the type of prosperous condition described in Ezekiel 38:12-13. These verses portray Israel as possessing a very robust economy.

More land, Jews, economic wealth, military strength and international influence should characterize Israel just before the Gog of Magog invasion. This burgeoning Israel should be bursting at the seams, which will be conducive to improved and expanded foreign relations with other countries. However, this won't be the case for the Muslim nations that survive the NOW prophetic scenarios, like Iran, Turkey, Libya etc. These countries will probably not be pleased with Israel after the fulfillment of several NOW Prophecies, like Psalm 83, (Arab-Israeli war), Isaiah 17, (destruction of Damascus), and Jeremiah 49:1-6, (toppling of Jordan).

Leading up to Ezekiel 38, the primary focus of the Muslim nations will be more on the defeat of their fellow Muslims by the IDF, than on the opportunities available to them through this new and improved Israel. Arab casualties of war, prisoners of war and displaced Muslim refugees, will contribute to their hatred toward Israel.

Israel should also be capturing war spoils, which could include increased territory. These spoils of war could be part of the plunder and booty described in Ezekiel 38:12-13. Israel has a pattern of territorial expansion after winning wars. Joshua did this about 3300 years ago. David and Solomon also did this about 3000 years ago. Israel did this in 1967 after the infamous "Six-Day" war.

Israel feels justified in seizing neighboring lands for two primary reasons. *First*, it is part of the land God gave to Abraham in Genesis 15:18. *Second*, because it increases the defensibility of their borders.

The Ezekiel 38 Muslim nations will also be upset with Israel if, after defeating the Arabs of Psalm 83, they break ground on the construction of their third Jewish temple. According to Bible prophecy, Israel will rebuild their temple sometime before the middle of the seven-year tribulation period. Today, the Temple Institute in Jerusalem declares that its ultimate goal is, "*To see Israel rebuild the Holy Temple on Mount Moriah in Jerusalem, in accord with the Biblical commandments.*"[2]

I point out later in this book, that it is likely that the coming Jewish Temple will be built after the fulfillment of the Psalm 83 and Ezekiel 38 wars. I present three scriptural clues that suggest the rebuilding of the Temple is permitted as part of Israel's participation in the false covenant of Isaiah 28:15-18 and Daniel 9:27.

Gog's evil plan

Although the surviving Muslim nations should be upset with Israel, and some Western nations supportive of the improved Israel, Russia will likely be jealous of the thriving Jewish state. A cruel Russian leader surfaces on the scene. We are informed in Ezekiel 38:10 that he devises a maniacal plan against Israel.

> 'Thus says the Lord GOD: "On that day it shall come to pass *that* thoughts will arise in your mind, and you will make an evil plan." (Ezek. 38:10)

Ezekiel 38:11-13 explains that the Russian leader's "evil plan" is to assemble a formidable strategic coalition in order to invade Israel for the sake of material gain. I point out the tactical aspect of his sinister plan in the chapter entitled "Russia Forms an Evil Plan to Invade Israel," in my book called *Revelation Road, Hope Beyond the Horizon*. The *Revelation Road* chapter posits the possibility that the Magog coalition is strategically assembled by Russia. Certain countries probably coalesce for one or more of the following reasons. Below is a quote from the *Revelation Road* book.

- *"Predominantly Muslim Nations opposed to Israel* - Apart from Russia, the other countries are predominantly Muslim. They are already spiritually united through their common faith. Although schisms exist between Sunni and Shia nations, they all share a common hatred of Israel. Most of the Ezekiel invaders including, Iran, Libya, Tunisia, Algeria, Morocco, Sudan and Somalia, currently refuse to recognize Israel as the Jewish state.[3]

- *Angry with Israel after Psalm 83* - Presently, these Islamic nations are not fond of Israel. Their disdain toward Israel will increase after the IDF conquers the Muslim confederacy described in Psalm 83.

- *Important Mideast Water Arteries*- The Ezekiel invaders all border the available waterways that Israel will need to export its commerce into world markets. This alignment of nations can blockade these important water arteries. Turkey, Libya, Tunisia and Algeria surround the Mediterranean Sea. Iran can blockade the Persian Gulf. Ethiopia and Somalia can hinder shipments passing through the Red Sea."

The formulation of the evil bent Magog coalition will ruffle more than Israel's feathers. The protestors identified in Ezekiel 38:13 along with other nations that are supportive of Israel will become extremely tense at the time. (*The identity of these protestors is provided within my NOW Prophecies book in the chapter called, "Is America in Ezekiel 38?"*).

All eyes throughout the world will undoubtedly be focused upon the mainstream news channels to see what Russia's evil intentions are. As the Magog coalition takes shape and begins to assemble to the north of Israel, according to Ezekiel 38:6, 15 and 39:2, the global audience will view the spectacle with bated breath. "*What in the world is Russia up to?*" They will wonder.

As the intent of the invaders becomes perfectly clear, the Muslim nations will mostly applaud or enlist in the coalition. However, the western world will adopt a different attitude. Considering the strong possibility that the Rapture may happen prior to the Ezekiel 38 invasion, the UK, EU and USA will probably be restricted to the role of protestors. The instantaneous unexplained disappearances of the Christians within their populations will present them with an overwhelming dilemma.

On the flip side, if the Rapture has occurred the Muslim nations should be reinvigorated because it will have a lesser impact on these countries than those with a Christian background. The Rapture involves only true believers, and although many Muslims are currently converting to Christianity, their homelands remain primarily Islamic.

Just when the hordes of Ezekiel 38 invaders are marching upon the soil of Israel, with all their weapons of warfare locked and loaded, something catches them completely off guard! Television viewers around the world become shocked to see that a massive earthquake rocks the area! The sequences of supernatural catastrophes that follow are explained in Ezekiel 38:14-39:8 and summarized sequentially below.

1. A great earthquake occurs in the land of Israel,
2. The mountains are thrown down,
3. The steep places fall, and every wall falls to the ground,
4. The Ezekiel invaders panic and kill one another, *"Every man's sword will be against his brother,"*
5. This brings about pestilence and bloodshed,
6. Then pelting rain pours down on the invading troops,
7. This causes severe flooding,
8. The rain manifests into great hailstones of fire, and brimstone.

What are the conditions in Israel during the invasion?

The previous few paragraphs along with those about to follow in this section are admittedly somewhat speculative. However, author liberties are being taken in order to paint a biblically based portrait of how the Ezekiel 38 invasion might unfold. You are encouraged to have your Bibles open to the pertinent passages to confirm that my interpretations are not too far-fetched.

Ezekiel 38:19-20 says there will be a *"great earthquake in the land of Israel."* The magnitude of the quake will cause all men upon the face of the whole earth to *"shake."* Affected *mountains* will crumble and *walls* will fall. When was the last time you saw mountains, (plural), topple as the result of an earthquake? Also, wonder who might be killed when the affected mountains are thrown down.

Imagine watching this spectacular scene that interrupts the advance of the Magog invaders on your TV set. What is about to follow is all supernatural. Neither the IDF, nor the American military plays any role in what happens next.

Ezekiel 38:21 declares that *"Every man's sword will be against his brother."* This is alluding to the Magog invaders. Apparently, the powerful repercussions from the seismic event causes panic among the troops, who then begin attacking one another. This is not an example of "friendly fire." This is an illustration of what happened in Israel's history when Gideon's 300- man army fought against the Midianites. Judges 7:22 says, *"the LORD set every man's sword against his companion throughout the whole camp."*

Ezekiel 38:22 informs, *"I will rain down on him, on his troops, and on the many peoples who are with him, flooding rain, great hailstones, fire, and brimstone."* As if the earthquake, which will topple mountains, crumble walls and result in the killing of one another wasn't enough, matters go from terrible to horrendous for the invaders. Flooding rains accompanied by stone size hailstones pummel the invaders. Fire and brimstone finish them off. By the time all the supernatural events above conclude,

1. The Magog invaders are destroyed,
2. The television watchers around the world are in shock,
3. And, Israel is counting their blessings and praising Jehovah the God of Abraham, Isaac and Jacob.

Ezekiel 39:1-6 provides more graphic details about what happens to the invaders and then Ezekiel 39:7-8 sheds light on the purpose of the experience.

> "So I will make My holy name known in the midst of My people Israel, and I will not *let them* profane My holy name anymore. Then the nations shall know that *I am* the LORD, the Holy One in Israel. Surely it is coming, and it shall be done," says the Lord GOD. "This *is* the day of which I have spoken." (Ezekiel 39:7-8)

It will be hard for anyone that watched or experienced this event first hand to walk away with any other conclusion than what is said in these two verses. This is how the Lord notifies the nations, including Israel, that He is the one true God, the upholder of the unconditional Abrahamic Covenant and the promise keeper of all believers.

Notice that the above verses read, "*the nations shall know that I am the LORD.*" Although the supernatural defeat of the Ezekiel invaders makes it evident that the God of the Bible is the LORD, it doesn't mean that mankind at large accepts the LORD. Several predictions that follow Ezekiel 38, like in the seventh bowl judgment of Revelation, point out that many people remain in rebellion against the LORD.

> The seventh bowl judgment: "*And great hail from heaven fell upon men, each hailstone* about the weight of a talent. Men blasphemed God because of the plague of the hail, since that plague was exceedingly great." (Rev. 16:21)

The great hail from this bowl judgment is not the same as that of Ezekiel 38:22. The Rev. 16:21 hail judgment happens near the end of the seven-year Tribulation, which is sometime after the destruction of the Ezekiel invaders.

What are the conditions in Israel in the aftermath?

Ezekiel 39:9-21 explains what happens in Israel in the aftermath of God's supernatural victory over the Magog invaders.

Israel uses the enemy's weapons

Ezekiel 39:9-10 clues us in to the types of weaponry the invaders possess. The weapons must be of the sort that Israel will be able to convert into fuel. Ezekiel says that "*they will make fire with them for seven years.*" The picture is of energy provision for the entire nation, rather than a few isolated households. Verse 9 says, "*those who dwell in the cities,*" utilize this converted weapons-grade fuel.

The use of the pronouns, "*they*" and "*those,*" identify the Israelis. It is the Israelis that are utilizing the left-over weapons of the invaders for civilian purposes. The Magog invaders intended to use the weapons for harm, but the Lord intends to use them for good.

The widespread use and lengthy seven-year span suggests that the weapons must be far more sophisticated than wooden bows and arrows, which would undoubtedly only last a short while. I mention this because some expositors today limit the weapons to wooden ones. I doubt nuclear non-proliferation will reduce Russian arsenals to wood between now and then. In fact, Russia is still building and testing new and improved nuclear weapons according to the July 19, 2018 headline from "The Hill" below.

"Russia announces new nuclear weapons tests days after Trump-Putin summit"

The missiles and rockets that are being converted to fuel in Ezekiel 39:9-10 probably include the ABCs of weaponry—atomic, biological, and chemical. We can presume this because these types of weapons already exist inside the arsenals of Russia and some of their cohorts. Additionally, the dead soldiers appear to require Hazmat (Hazardous Materials) teams to assist with their burial according to Ezekiel 39:14-16. The fascinating fact is that whatever the weapons configuration, Israel will possess the technological know-how to convert them into national energy. Today, whether it is cell phones or irrigation techniques, Israel is on the cutting-edge of technological advances.

The Magog invaders intended to use these weapons to dispossess Israel of its booty, which would include its energy resources, but the opposite occurs. Israel converts the enemy weaponry into additional energy sources for themselves, instead of having their energy sources stolen.

Israel buries the Magog invaders

Ezekiel 39:11-16 describes the location of the mass burial grounds of the destroyed armies of Gog. A valley east of what is probably the Dead Sea is renamed the Valley of Hamon Gog, which means the "hordes or multitudes" of Gog, in Hebrew. Why I believe it refers to a valley in modern-day Jordan is explained in the chapter called, "Greater Israel," of my *Psalm 83: The Missing Prophecy Revealed, How Israel Becomes the Next Mideast Superpower* book.

We also find in Ezekiel 39:11-16 that the Israelis will be burying the dead in order to cleanse the land. This could imply two things. *One*, that the hordes of Gog's dead soldiers are contaminated, which would require a professional quarantined burial. This contamination could come from either the fallout from their atomic, biological and / or chemical weapons, or the deteriorating corpses strewn across the battlefield. *Two*, the Jews are adhering to their ancient Levitical Law according to Numbers 19:11-22 and Deuteronomy 21:1-9. These verses set forth specifications about the appropriate handling of dead bodies lying on the land of Israel.

Ezekiel 39:17-20 is an invitation "to every sort of bird and to every beast of the field" to partake of the sacrificial meal of the "flesh" and "blood" of the invaders. This passage is not for the faint of heart. Some try to connect this feast with the similar sacrificial meal described in Revelation 19:17-18, but there are stark differences.

1.   Ezekiel's sacrificial meal involves the death of Gog, a Russian leader, but the Revelation 19 account is dealing with the Antichrist of European descent, who according to Daniel 9:26 comes out of the revived Roman Empire.
2.   Ezekiel's meal is dealing with the carnage of only the Gog of Magog invaders, but the Revelation scenario includes, "*the flesh of kings, the flesh of captains, the flesh of mighty men, the flesh of horses and of those who sit on them, and the flesh of all people free and slave, both small and great.*"

Ezekiel 39:21-29 concludes the chapter with a recap of some Jewish history and a promise to the faithful remnant of Israel that the Lord will pour out His spirit upon them in the end. The Holy Spirit will be bestowed to the faithful remnant when they recognize Christ as their Messiah. This is one of the rewards for believing in Jesus Christ. (John 14:16-17, 26, 15:26, 16:7).

INTERESTING OBSERVANCE: The Ezekiel 39:17 birds of prey appear to be already gathering in Israel. This implies that the Ezekiel 38 invasion, which concludes with the sacrificial meal, draws near. If this is the case, this makes sense because the local birds, rather than those that have to migrate from great distances, would be the immediate benefactors of the sacrificial feast. Some interesting headlines below reference the increased bird populations existing in Israel.[4]

- May 14, 2007, *Haaretz* – "The Iraqi Bird(s) That Made Aliyah (to Israel)."

- January 25, 2012, *Haaretz* – "Long-lost Starlings Are Flying Back to Israel."

- February 26, 2016, *Times of Israel* – "Why Israel is a pilgrimage site for birds and bird-watchers."

- January 23, 2017, *Haaretz* – "Israel's 500 Million Birds: The World's Eighth Wonder."

- April 25, 2017, *Jerusalem Post* – "Bird Makes a Rare Stop in Israel After Wrong Turn."

- July 24, 2017, *Jerusalem Post* – "Israeli Vulture Population on the Rise."

Summary

Ezekiel 38 and 39 provides some of the most important, well explained, and easy to understand prophecies in the Bible. This is because these chapters foretell of the coming marquis event, whereby the Lord upholds His holy name before the watchful eyes of humankind. The event is so epic that the Lord achieves the undivided attention of mankind. Israelis continuing to inhabit their homeland of Israel, after the prophetic wars of Psalm 83 and Ezekiel 38, will provide humanity with ample evidence to recognize that the God of the Bible is the one true God!

The timing of Ezekiel 38 is critical. It occurs in the end times when the Promised Land of Israel hosts the Chosen People

(Israelis). The Rapture of the church could occur before, during or after the event. My personal view is that the Ezekiel 38 is a NEXT Prophecy that occurs after the Rapture, but prior to the seven-year Tribulation period. I non-dogmatically believe that Ezekiel 38 finds fulfillment prior to the implementation of the Antichrist's "Mark of the Beast" campaign in Revelation 13:11-18.

Topics related to the Timing of Ezekiel 38

Below are a few of my reasons for adopting the post-Rapture, but Pre-Tribulation gap. view for the timing of Ezekiel 38.

1. *My people Israel* – God calls the Israelis "My people Israel" three times in Ezekiel 38 and 39. (Ezekiel 38:14, 16 and 39:7). This suggests that the true believers within the Church need not be present. This is all about Israel and the Israelis. This is one reason I believe the Rapture could occur before Ezekiel 38 finds fulfillment.
2. *Upholding His Holy name* – The fact that the Lord chooses this end time's episode to uphold His holy name suggests that timing is important. Demonstrating His holiness by delivering Israel from the most massive Mideast invasion in all of history up to that point, gives humanity the opportunity to believe in God before being deceived by the Antichrist. The Antichrist becomes a central figure throughout the seven-year Tribulation period. He rises to power through great deception according to 2 Thessalonians 2:8-12. A Pre-Tribulation fulfillment of Ezekiel 38 provides people with a clear choice between believing in the holy promise keeping God of the Bible, or the unholy deceiver, the Antichrist.
3. *Israel burns weapons for seven years* – in addition to the reason above, I hold to the teaching that Ezekiel 39:9-10 presents another clue to the timing of Ezekiel 38 and 39.

"Then those who dwell in the cities of Israel will go out and set on fire and burn the weapons, both the shields and bucklers, the bows and arrows, the javelins and spears; and they will make fires with them for seven years. They will not take wood from the field nor cut down *any* from the forests, because they will make fires with the weapons; and they will plunder those who plundered them, and pillage those who pillaged them," says the Lord GOD." (Ezek. 39:9-10)

These Ezekiel verses say that Israelis, "those who dwell in the cities of Israel," will make fires with the enemy's weapons. Israelis appear to utilize these weapons for energy consumption for a period of seven-years. This will be no problem during the peaceful first half of the tribulation, but not likely during the perilous second half, because Jews will be fleeing for their lives, rather than harnessing this energy.

Concerning the separation point between the first and second halves of the Trib-period, Christ warned the Israelis in Matthew 24:15-22 that they should flee for their lives when they witness the "abomination of desolation," because that signaled a period of "Great Tribulation" was coming. This abominable event occurs at the mid-point of the Tribulation period.

"Therefore when you see the *'abomination of desolation,'* spoken of by Daniel the prophet, standing in the holy place" (whoever reads, let him understand), "then let those who are in Judea flee to the mountains. Let him who is on the housetop not go down to take anything out of his house. And let him who is in the field not go back to get his clothes. But woe to those who are pregnant and to those who are nursing babies in those days! And pray that your flight may not be in winter or on the Sabbath. For then there will be great tribulation, such as has not been since the beginning of the world until this time, no, nor ever shall be. And unless those days were shortened, no flesh would be saved; but for the elect's sake those days will be shortened." (Matthew 24:15-22)

These Matthew 24 verses are part of the reason the second half of the Tribulation is commonly called the Great Tribulation. It stands to reason that if Christ instructs Israelis to flee immediately for safety at the midpoint of the Tribulation period that the refugees won't be stopping along the way to convert anymore of these weapons in the process. If anything, they might pick up a weapon to use it, rather than burn it.

Therefore, many scholars suggest that Ezekiel 38 and 39 must conclude, not commence, no later than three and one-half years before the seven-years of tribulation even begins. This allows the Jews seven full years to burn the weapons before they begin fleeing for their lives.

3

Introduction to the Post-Rapture /Pre-Tribulation Gap Period

One of the most important teachings within this book is that a time-gap exists between the Rapture of the Church and the start of the seven-year Tribulation Period. For the purposes of this book, this period is referred to as the Post-Rapture / Pre-Tribulation gap period. This time-gap begins in the immediate aftermath of the Rapture, which positions it in the Post-Rapture period. However, it concludes at the commencement point of the seven-year Trib-period, making it a Pre-Tribulation interval.

This time-gap hypothesis is based upon the premise that it's not the Rapture that triggers the start of the Trib-period, but it is the confirmation of a covenant by the Antichrist between Israel and some other party or parties that triggers the ticking of the Trib-period. This covenant is identified primarily in Daniel 9:27 and Isaiah 28:15 and 18.

In early 2011, I had the honor of receiving a personal email from the late Bible prophecy expert, Tim LaHaye (1926-2016), in which he shared his thoughts with me about this topic. His comments are below.

> *"Pre-Trib. scholars are not agreed on whether the rapture starts the Tribulation (Nothing in scripture says it does). Daniel 9:27 says the Antichrist will confirm a contract with Israel for one week (or*

seven years), which leads me to believe that starts the Tribulation. There is a high possibility that the Rapture could take place prior, but only God knows how long."

In this personal email above Dr. LaHaye admits to the possibility that a gap exists between the Rapture and the Tribulation period. Another interesting quote about the time-gap theory is below from Dr. David Reagan, the founder of Lamb and Lion Ministries. Dr. Reagan suggests this Post-Rapture gap could last for *"months or even years."* This quote was taken from his article review of my book called, *Apocalypse Road, Revelation for the Final Generation.*

"The second (book) in the (Salus book) series (entitled), Apocalypse Road: Revelation for the Final Generation (2017), focuses on the gap period between the Rapture and the beginning of the Tribulation. This is a much needed study since most people seem to assume that the Tribulation begins immediately after the Rapture. The fact of the matter is that the Tribulation is triggered by the Antichrist confirming a covenant made with Israel, and that could happen months or even years after the Rapture."[5]

Since the time-gap won't happen until after the Rapture, this makes this Post-Rapture / Pre-Tribulation gap period and all the prophecies described in this book that might occur within it, NEXT Prophecies. This means that the Rapture could be a significant pre-condition for some of the NEXT Prophecies!

In addition to Dr. Tim LaHaye and Dr. David Reagan, there are many other prophecy teachers that believe in a gap between the Rapture and the Tribulation period such as Gary Stearman, Billy Crone, Chuck Missler, Grant Jeffrey, Joel Rosenberg, Dr. Ron Rhodes, and Dr. Mark Hitchcock. However, there are some other prophecy teachers namely, Perry Stone, Jack Van Impe and

J. Vernon McGee, who don't believe in a gap theory. They believe that immediately after the Rapture, the tribulation period begins. This is pointed out in the book by Dr. F Kenton Beshore and R William Keller entitled, *When?: When Will The Rapture Take Place?*

Beshore and Keller, who don't believe in a time-gap, explain in their book that a primary basis for no gap is based upon the historic premise that on the very day when Noah entered the ark the flood judgment came and on the same day when Lot left Sodom and Gomorrah these two cities were destroyed. They use these two historic episodes as examples that foreshadow the Pre-Tribulation Rapture.

The no-gap premise fails to take into consideration the following important things,

1. It's not the Rapture that starts the Tribulation period, rather it's the confirmation of the false covenant in Daniel 9:27.
2. Noah was not Raptured, rather he went through the flood. Thus he is not a foreshadow of the Rapture. However, his great grandfather Enoch represents a picture of the Rapture. Enoch, while still being alive, was caught up to be with the Lord in Genesis 5:21-24. The departure of Enoch occurred well in advance of the flood judgment. A time-gap existed between Enoch's disappearance and the flood of Noah. This past event suggests that a Post-Rapture / Pre-Tribulation time-gap exists.
3. In the example of Lot with the judgment upon Sodom and Gomorrah, the destruction was immediate. However the outpouring of God's wrath during the Tribulation period spans seven-years. The Antichrist doesn't even implement his "Mark of the Beast" cashless society of Revelation chapter 13 until three and one-half years into the seven-year period. Although, this beastly system gets destroyed in one-hour according to Revelation 18:10-19, this destruction doesn't take place until the end of the Tribulation period.

The remainder of this book attempts to accomplish the following:

1. List and chronologically order the potential prophecies that fit into the Post-Rapture / Pre-Tribulation gap period, or maybe within the first half of the seven-year Tribulation Period.

2. Determine how long the gap period could be from the clues provided in the prophecies that find fulfillment within this vastly overlooked period.

3. Set the world stage as it transitions from the Church age, which concludes with the Rapture, into the gap period that follows.

4. Explore the timing of first five seals of Revelation 6:1-11 and explain their potential meanings. This includes;

    a. Introduce the Antichrist as the white horseman of the Apocalypse, (Rev. 6:1-2),

    b. Examine the wars that plague the planet through the fiery red horseman of the Apocalypse, (Rev. 6:3-4),

    c. Warn about the wide scale famines, pestilences, and economic upheavals that occur during the ride of the black horseman of the Apocalypse, (Rev. 6:5-6),

    d. Put a face on the fourth horsemen of Death and Hades of the Apocalypse, (Rev. 6:7-8),

    e. Reveal the identities of the three primary groups of martyred believers after the Rapture, which are the fifth seal saints, their fellow servants and their brethren, (Rev. 6:11).

5. Identify Roman Catholicism as "Mystery, Babylon The Great, The Mother Of Harlots And Abominations Of The Earth" of Revelation 17:5.

6. Determine who the two parties are to the seven-year covenant that starts the Trib-period.

7. Define the *true content* on what is commonly called the *false covenant* of Daniel 9:27, as it pertains to the "overflowing scourge," of Isaiah 28:15 and 18.

8. Explain the two judgments of end times Babylon.
9. *Most importantly*, the sincerest goal of this timely and unique work is to forewarn and prepare EVERYONE for the SOON ARRIVAL of this treacherous Post-Rapture / Pre-Tribulation gap period!

Conclusion

Many readers will get Raptured as true believers of Jesus Christ before this gap period commences. The good news is that they will not personally face the frightening events that are forthcoming in the gap period. The bad news is that someone they love will!

This work has been specifically designed to stimulate the mind and pulsate the heart of believers, and to invigorate their love for the lost. Careful consideration in that regard has gone into the overall content of this entire composition. If you are concerned about the eternal destiny of an unsaved loved one, then consider this book as your invaluable instruction manual for these last days. The biblically supported scenarios within this book will embolden you to share the good news about Jesus Christ with the ones you love.

4

What Will the World Look Like Shortly After the Rapture?

After the Rapture, humankind will enter a new era. The paranormal will become the new normal, the supernatural will swiftly seem more natural, and what was once considered futuristic rapidly becomes very realistic. This is because the Rapture is a miraculous event and Satan immediately follows it up with powerful lying signs and wonders.

The worldwide disappearances of millions of believers will likely warrant more than a simple scientific explanation. The spiritual and prophetic implications surrounding the event will necessitate a religious response. Satan realizes this and, after the Rapture, he has a campaign filled with supernatural surprises ready to be promptly put in place. According to 2 Thessalonians 2:6-7, nothing after the Rapture will hinder the double religious jeopardy that the Devil has prepared to deceive mankind. I consider these 2 Thessalonians verses to be dealing with significant NEXT Prophecies.

First, the Harlot world religion of Revelation 17 will surface and after it has overextended its usefulness, it becomes desolated by the "Ten Kings" in Revelation 17:16. This appears to happen at the mid-point of the Trib-period, which means that the reign of this false global religion likely begins during the gap period, but concludes in the middle of the Trib-period. When the Harlot is dethroned, the Antichrist becomes fully enthroned. He hails over the second global system described in Revelation 13. Satan has devised a one-two punch that people left behind won't likely expect, but many sadly will accept.

In the immediate aftermath of the Rapture, the world will become increasing unruly as lawlessness is predicted to increase. Wars occur as world peace departs as per the opening of the second seal in Revelation 6:3-4, which is a NEXT Prophecy. These catastrophic global conditions facilitate the emergence of the "Lawless One," which is another title of the Antichrist. His introduction into the world theater is among the first order of events to occur after the Rapture. This crazed world leader is the White Horseman of the Apocalypse described in the first seal in Rev. 6:1-2, another NEXT Prophecy.

All the things described in the above paragraph closely parallel the predicted events in the 2 Thessalonians 2 verses below.

Do you not remember that when I was still with you I told you these things? And now you know what is restraining, that he may be revealed in his own time. For the mystery of lawlessness is already at work; only He who now restrains (*lawlessness*) *will do so* until He is taken out of the way. And then the lawless one (*Antichrist*) will be revealed, whom the Lord (*Jesus Christ*) will consume with the breath of His mouth and destroy with the brightness of His coming. The coming of the *lawless one* is according to the working of Satan, with all power, signs, and lying wonders, and with all unrighteous deception among those who perish, because they did not receive the love of the truth, that they might be saved. (2 Thessalonians 2:5-10; emphasis added)

Summary: The World Shortly After the Rapture

With the disappearances of believers, the world clock nears midnight. Ancient biblical prophecies, which were intended to be fulfilled in the last days, will begin to roll off their parchments and pound onto the pavement in relatively rapid succession. Each one has the potential to pack a more powerful punch than the one that preceded it.

Many people who were left behind will wonder where the believers went. As they attempt to return to their normal lives, a paranormal reality promises them an uncertain future. Global chaos will be mounting, which will necessitate the formation of a world government to restore international order. The stage will be set for Satan to send his point man, the Antichrist, into the world theater, and that's exactly what he does!

5

The Church is in Heaven Before the Antichrist is Revealed on Earth

One of the first Next Prophecies that happens after the Rapture is the revealing of the Antichrist. The consensus among many Bible prophecy experts is that he shows up with the opening of the first seal.

> Now I saw when the Lamb opened one of the seals; and I heard one of the four living creatures saying with a voice like thunder, "Come and see." And I looked, and behold, a white horse. He who sat on it had a bow; and a crown was given to him, and he went out conquering and to conquer. (Revelation 6:1-2) (A NEXT Prophecy).

Some confuse the rider of this white horse with Jesus Christ, Who is also pictured riding a white horse in Revelation 19:11. However, the white horseman of the first seal judgment is different. Below is a quote from "The Bible Knowledge Commentary New Testament by, John Walvoord and Roy B. Zuck.

> *Revelation 6:1-2 – "As John watched the events after the opening of the first... seal by the Lamb, he saw a white horse with a rider holding a bow, wearing a victor's crown (stephanos), and going*

forth to conquer. Because Christ in His second coming is pictured (19:11) as riding on a white horse, some have taken it that this rider in 6:2 also must refer to Christ, as the white horse is a symbol of victory. Roman generals after a victory in battle would ride a white horse in triumph with their captives following. The chronology, however, is wrong, as Christ returns to the earth as a conqueror not at the beginning of the Tribulation but at the end of the Tribulation. Also, the riders on the other horses obviously relate to destruction and judgment which precede the second coming of Christ by some period of time."

There are at least two important questions to ask and address concerning the opening of the first seal judgment.

1.   Question: *When is the first seal opened?*
     Answer: Probably in the early stages after the Rapture of the Church.

2.   Question: *Does the Trib-period begin when the first seal is opened?*
     Answer: Maybe not...

This topic is explored in greater detail in the coming chapters called, "The Traditional View of the Seal Judgments of Revelation 6," and "The Alternative View of the Seal Judgments of Revelation 6." However, this brief section below explains why the opening of the first seal could happen in the gap period and does not likely trigger the start of the seven-year Trib-period. These conclusions are supported by the following reasons below.

First, the church is pictured in heaven before the first seal is opened, which means that the Rapture has previously occurred. This point is explained later in this chapter. *Second,* the Antichrist's rise to political power takes time. *Third,* the other party to the false covenant of Daniel 9:27 factors into prophecy after the first seal has already been opened. This book will point out why the other signatory to the false covenant doesn't seem to appear on earth until the fourth Seal of Revelation 6 is opened.

The theory is that the Trib-period doesn't commence until after this false covenant is made between Israel and another party. The role of the Antichrist in this scenario is to confirm this covenant between the two parties. Israel is one of the parties and Daniel 9:27 informs that other party is called "many." Who the "many" probably represents is explored later within this book.

The Christian Church is residing in heaven before the tribulation period commences. This conclusion is supported by understanding the chronological ordering of chapters two through six in the book of Revelation. Revelation 2 and 3 describe the Church on earth while Revelation 4 and 5 pictures the Church residing in heaven. Revelation 6 introduces the earthly events that occur after the Christian Church has been removed from the earth via the Rapture. The prophecies in Revelation 6 segue into the Trib-period. The details of this ordering are explained below.

Revelation 2 and 3 contain the seven letters to the seven Churches. These letters had multiple applications at the time of their issuance. They had a literal, allegorical and prophetic usages. First, literally they provided important individualized information for the seven specific Churches that they were addressed to. These Churches all existed at that time. Second, allegorically these letters detailed the distinguishing characteristics that would exist at any given time within various Churches throughout the Church age. Third, they prophetically outlined the future of the Church age. These two chapters portrayed the overall Christian Church during its existence on earth during the Church age from its inception until its completion. More information on this topic is provided in the Appendix entitled, "*The Seven Letters to the Churches.*"

After the Church age represented in Revelation 2 and 3 is completed, meaning once it is removed from the earth via the Rapture, Revelation 4 begins. Revelation 4 starts with the Greek words *"meta tauta,"* which means *"after these things."* After what things? After the events in Revelation chapters 2 and 3 have prophetically occurred. Then, the Church is caught up to heaven and pictured there in Revelation 4 and 5.

> "After these things (*meta tauta*) I (*the apostle John*) looked, and behold, a door standing open in heaven. And the first voice which I heard was like a trumpet speaking with me, saying, "Come up here, [*representing the rapture*] and I will show you things which must take place after this." (Revelation 4:1, NKJV; emphasis added).

Further evidence that the Church is in heaven in Revelation 4 and 5 concerns the identity of the twenty-four elders. It is commonly taught that these twenty-four elders represent the Church in heaven. Revelation 5:9 informs that these elders are redeemed by the blood of Christ. Only true believers are qualified to make such a salvation claim. Moreover, these redeemed individuals are *"out of every tribe and tongue and people and nation."* This appears to be an acknowledgement that they likely represent the believers saved throughout the world during the Church age.

Quoted below, is how noted Bible prophecy scholar Dr. Arnold Fruchtenbaum interprets the identity of the twenty-four elders

> *"While the text does not clearly state as to what these twenty-four elders refer, there are clues in the text by which their identity can be deduced. First, these elders are clothed with white garments, which throughout the Revelation are symbols of salvation. Celestial beings before the throne*

of God do not need salvation for they were not lost to begin with. But these elders were at one time lost and at some point received salvation as is seen by their wearing of the white garments. The second clue is the fact that they are wearing crowns. These crowns are not diadem crowns worn by those who are royal by nature, which would have been the case had these been celestial beings. These crowns are the stephanos crowns, the crowns of an overcomer; the type of crown given as rewards to the members of the church at the Judgment Seat of Christ. A third clue lies in their very title of elders. Nowhere else in Scripture is this term used to describe celestial or angelic beings. This term is used of humans in positions of authority either in the synagogue or church. Hence, from these three clues, the twenty-four elders must represent the church saints. If this is true, then they provide further evidence for a pre-tribulation Rapture. The church is already in heaven in chapter four and five before the tribulation begins in chapter six."[6]

Sometime after the Church gets caught up into heaven in Revelation 4, the events described in Revelation 5 commence. One very significant event that the twenty-four elders witness is the opening of the heavenly scroll by Jesus Christ. This scroll contains the seven seal judgments. As previously pointed out, the first seal judgment introduces the Antichrist upon the earth. As per Daniel 9:27, the Antichrist confirms a covenant with Israel for seven years. It is commonly taught that the ratification and implementation of this covenant becomes the starting point of the seven years of the tribulation period.

Therefore, it can be concluded that only when the Church resides in heaven, can it watch Christ open the scroll that contains the seven seal judgments. Until these seal judgments are opened, the Antichrist can't emerge upon the world scene and confirm the seven-year covenant with Israel. As long as the covenant can't be confirmed, the tribulation period can't commence.

In summary, the sequence of events are as follows;

1.   The Church gets caught up to heaven,
2.   Upon entering heaven, the Church, represented as the twenty-four elders, witnesses Jesus Christ open the heavenly scroll that contains the seven seal judgments,
3.   The Antichrist arrives on the world stage when the seal judgments are opened,
4.   At some point after the Antichrist arrives he confirms a covenant between Israel and another party or parties,
5.   This is when the tribulation period commences.

6

Introducing
the Antichrist

2 Thessalonians 2:5-10, which was previously quoted, pointed out that the "lawless one," i.e. the Antichrist, can't be revealed until the restrainer is removed.

> For the mystery of lawlessness is already at work; only He (*the one presently restraining lawlessness*) who now restrains *will do so* until He is taken out of the way. And then the lawless one (*the Antichrist*) will be revealed, whom the Lord (*Jesus Christ*) will consume with the breath of His mouth and destroy with the brightness of His (*second*) coming. (2 Thess. 2:7-8; emphasis added)

Some Bible teachers, myself included, correlate the timing of the Rapture with the removal of the restrainer. Presently, the Holy Spirit appears to be multi-tasking. He is reconciling believers to God and restraining the mystery of lawlessness.

2 Thessalonians 2 appears to inform that the Church is Raptured, the restraint of lawlessness is removed, and promptly afterward the Antichrist is revealed. The timing of these events chronologically coincides with the timing of Revelation 4, (the Rapture), Revelation 5, (the presentation of the heavenly scroll) and Revelation 6, (the opening of the seals and the arrival of the Antichrist).

The Mystery of Lawlessness and the Lawless One

There are at least three mysteries exposed in the New Testament that find a Pre-Tribulation period fulfillment. One of them happens before the gap period as a Now Prophecy, the Rapture, and the other two appear to begin in the gap period as Next Prophecies, Lawlessness and Mystery Babylon. These three are, the Mysteries of the Rapture, (1 Corinthians 15:51), Lawlessness, (2 Thess. 2:7), and Babylon, (Revelation 17:5, 7). Once the Rapture becomes a reality, the stage is set for the fulfillment of the other two. The "mystery of lawlessness" is presented here because it is relevant to the timing of the revealing of the "lawless one."

The Greek word for mystery is "*musterion*," and it is translated as a mystery or secret doctrine.[7] Lawlessness, also translated as iniquity in some translations, is the Greek word, "*anomia*." It is used 13 times in the New Testament. It is defined as sin in 1 John 3:4. However, the fact that lawlessness is sin is not a mystery. So, the question arises; why did the apostle Paul label lawlessness as a mystery?

The common interpretation of a biblical mystery is that it is something that was not disclosed in the Old Testament, but is now exposed in the New Testament. A mystery in this case is information that is solely privy to God until He makes it known to the public, through the Holy Scriptures. Some mysteries deal with future events. Once the future episode finds fulfillment, it becomes a reality and ceases from further being a mystery. It becomes an actuality to the generation that witnesses its fulfillment. For instance, once the Rapture happens, it can no longer be classified as a mystery because it has become a historical fact.

A summary of what lawlessness is, as per its thirteen usages in the New Testament, is provided below.

Lawlessness is the opposite of righteousness, (2 Corinthians 6:14). It is an integral part of Satan's end time scheme, (2 Thess. 2:1-10). It characterized the condition of the scribes and Pharisees at the time of the first coming of Christ, (Matthew 23: 27-28). Similarly, it becomes implanted into the Kingdom of God prior to the second coming of Christ. Like tares adversely affect the wheat during harvest time, Satan uses lawlessness as a stumbling block to harm the people of God in the last days, (Matt. 13:36-43). When lawlessness goes unrestrained in the end times, it metastasizes into its most cancerous condition, causing the love of many throughout the world to grow cold, (Matt. 24:12). Its only cure is forgiveness through Jesus Christ, (Romans 4:7, Hebrews 10:17).

Lawlessness is so bad that it must be restrained, for the overall good of the Church while it exists upon the earth. The Church is not appointed to experience lawlessness when it spreads throughout the world without further hindrance, and that's why it is Raptured out beforehand. As per 1 Thess. 5:9, the Church is likewise not appointed to the wrath of God, however lawlessness is not poured out by God, rather it is unleashed according to the working of Satan, with all power, signs, and lying wonders, and with all unrighteous deception among those who perish, (2 Thess. 2:9-10; abbreviated).

A lawless world provides the ideal environment through which the seed of Satan can incubate. The seed of Satan is another name for the Antichrist used in Genesis 3:15. Therefore, the lawless one is introduced into the end times equation in the immediate aftermath of the removal of the restraint of lawlessness. With the opening of the first 5 seal judgments, lawlessness no longer remains a mystery, but becomes a global reality. The breakdown goes as follows;

1. The Lawless one arrives on the global stage with the opening of the first seal, which evidences that lawlessness is no longer restrained, but is dispersing rapidly throughout the world,
2. This unhindered spread of evil disrupts world peace, giving rise to war(s) as per the second seal,
3. Impoverished conditions plague the planet with scarcities, famines and pestilences because of the first two seals, during the third seal,

4.   A global government, which is made up of an unholy Church and State alliance, forms to remedy the dire situation in the fourth seal,
5.   True believers, called the fifth seal saints, get martyred for their Christian testimonies by the global government of the fourth seal, which is perpetrating lawlessness and suppressing the truth about Christ. God allows these believers to die for their faith, because He is no longer restraining lawlessness, like He did during the Church Age. In Revelation 6:11, 13:10 and 14:12, Jesus instructs His Post-Rapture followers to be patient until He physically returns in His second coming.

The Antichrist's Rise to Political Power Takes Time

One of the reasons that the seven-year Trib-period might not start immediately upon the opening of the first seal is because, it will require some time for the Antichrist to accomplish his three-fold career of becoming a political, military and religious leader.

Additionally, there exists nowhere in the text of Revelation 6:1-2, concerning the world debut of the Antichrist, any specific language about him confirming the covenant of Daniel 9:27. The Greek word that would best describe this covenant is "diatheke." This word for covenant is utilized 31 times in the New Testament, but is not used in Rev. 6:1-2.

Yet, the arrival of the Antichrist in the opening of the first seal is what causes many Bible prophecy teachers to conclude, that this must be where the Trib-period starts. These points are expounded upon in the two upcoming chapters dealing with the seal judgments. These chapters compare the traditional view of the seal judgments with an alternative view of the seal judgements.

Revelation 6:2 says that the Antichrist goes forth "conquering and to conquer." The dual usage of the word conquer, implies that the Antichrist embarks upon a process, which eventually over an unspecified time-period, accomplishes his three-fold career.

This conclusion is further supported by Revelation 17:3, 7, which predicts that at the initial stages of the Antichrist's career, he forms an unholy alliance with the Harlot world religion. These verses denote that the Antichrist allows the Harlot to "*sit*" on him, while he "*carries*" her to the heights of her position of becoming the predominate world religion. The Antichrist plays a subservient role to the Harlot, until he is ready to exert his dominance over the world. The relationship between the Harlot and the Antichrist is covered in greater detail in several different sections of commentary within this book.

As the Antichrist ascends to the heights of his political career, at some point along the way he earns the respect of Israel and the other party to the false covenant. They entrust him with the important responsibility of "confirming" the covenant between them. It is not until then, that the seven-years of tribulation begins.

When the Antichrist rises to power, he will attempt to end every other religion and pedestal his own. The apostle Paul calls him the "Son of Perdition" and informs us in 2 Thessalonians 2:4 that he is the one,

> "who opposes and exalts himself above all that is
> called God or that is worshiped, so that he sits
> as God in the (Third Jewish) temple of God,
> showing himself that he is God."

It is safe to presume that the spiritual system introduced by the Antichrist, which is propelled into position supernaturally by Satan through powerful deceptive wonders and lying signs, will be unlike anything before. It may incorporate some old pagan religious beliefs and practices, but it will likely include new concepts as well.

Some suggest it could be a new age spiritual movement that could include things like;

- Proof that mankind is not alone in this universe,

- Alien beings created mankind and influenced ancient religions, (These would likely be fallen angels, masquerading around as benevolent alien beings),

- How a person can become a god,

- And, how to achieve super human psychic abilities.

Whatever deceptive trappings come wrapped up in this final scheme, they will be effective in bringing many people to a belief in the Antichrist as the god above all gods.

The Three-Fold Career of the Antichrist.

Someday and somehow, Satan will introduce himself to his "seed" of Genesis 3:15. In my book entitled, *Apocalypse Road, Revelation for the Final Generation*, I created a fascinating fictitious scenario about how this might happen.

Ultimately, the Antichrist rises to political prominence, military power and religious dominance through a process of time. Rev. 6:2 says that he goes forth "*conquering and to conquer.*" The Greek word *nikaoô* is repeated in this verse. In addition to "conquering and to conquer," the word can be translated to *prevail, overcome, overpower* or be victorious.[8]

The Antichrist will *prevail* politically, *overcome* militarily and *overpower* religiously. He will become victorious in these three important arenas. He is wearing a stefanos crown, which is a wreath or crown of victory. It is the type of crown that was awarded to a victor in the ancient athletic games, like the Greek Olympics.[9] Thus, he is victorious when he goes forth *conquering and to conquer.*

He prevails politically in Daniel 9:26-27 as the future prince, (political leader), that is called upon to confirm the all-important false covenant between Israel and another party. Modern day comparisons of a political leader possessing similar respect would be US Presidents Jimmy Carter and Bill Clinton, who were called upon to confirm covenants between Israel and Egypt, (Carter), and Israel and Jordan, (Clinton).

As a powerful political leader, he achieves military power. In Daniel 11:40, he is waging and winning major wars. Once he achieves both political and military power, he uses them to springboard into religious dominance. This is understood in the sequence of verses below.

1. Revelation 17:3, 7 – The Antichrist, as the beast, is pictured in an unholy church and state relationship with the harlot world religion. He appears to be somewhat subservient to the Harlot, in that she *"sits" on him* in verse 3, and he *"carries" her* to her religious heights in verse 7.
2. Daniel 9:27 – As stated above, this verse evidences that the Antichrist becomes the esteemed political leader who Israel and some other party called "many," possibly alluding to the Harlot, trust to confirm a seven-year covenant between them.
3. Revelation 17:12, 16 – These verses state that the Antichrist will join forces with ten kings, who then desolate the harlot world religious system.
4. 2 Thessalonians 2:4 and Daniel 11:36-39 – These verses explain that the Antichrist will go into the third Jewish Temple and exalt himself above every god, so that he shows himself as god. This happens after the harlot world religion is eliminated.
5. Daniel 7:24-25 – These verses describe that three of the ten kings, who were aligned with the Antichrist when the harlot world religion was desolated, decide to come against the Antichrist shortly thereafter. They

appear to rebel against his claims to be god. As such, the Antichrist subdues them.

6.   Daniel 11:40-41 – These verses seem to explain how two of the three kings, the king of the South and the king of the North, are subdued by being defeated in a war with the Antichrist.

7.   Revelation 13 – This chapter says that the Antichrist is afflicted with a mortal head wound. Thus, he appears to die. However, he then appears to resurrect from the dead, at which point, the world at large begins to worship him. The mortal wound might result from a war between one of the three subdued kings.

The various stages in which the Antichrist rises to power, *"conquering and to conquer,"* occur after the Rapture of the Church. Earlier in this book, I explained how the Church is pictured dwelling on earth in Revelation 2-3 and Raptured up into heaven in Revelation 4-5. It is from the vantage point of being in heaven that the Christian Church experiences Christ receiving the scroll in Revelation 5:7-8, and opening it in Revelation 6:1 to reveal the seven-seal judgments.

The first stage, which is predominately dealing with his political and military empowerment, occurs after the Rapture on up to the middle of the Trib-period. The second stage, which involves all three-fold aspects of his ascent, occurs in the second half of the Trib-period. His religious mission commences around the middle of the Trib-period after the Harlot is removed and he subsequently enters the Jewish Temple. By that time, Satan will have fully convinced the Antichrist that he is god and is worthy of worldwide worship. Revelation 13 details the religious aspect of the Antichrist's career.

The predominant and traditional teaching of the origin of the Antichrist is that he will come out of the Revived Roman Empire. This is what I, along with Dr. David Reagan, Dr. Arnold Fruchtenbaum, Dr. Ron Rhodes, Dr. Mark Hitchcock and a host of others believe. However, some, like Joel Richardson and Walid Shoebat, believe that the Antichrist will be a Muslim. A few others have entertained the possibility that he might be a Nephilim. Whatever his origin, he comes out of the Revived Roman Empire according to Daniel.

> "And after the sixty-two weeks Messiah (*Christ*) shall be cut off, (*Crucified*) but not for Himself; (*But, for the sins of mankind*) And the people (*Romans*) of the prince (*Antichrist*) who is to come Shall destroy the city (*Jerusalem*) and the sanctuary, (*Second Jewish Temple*). The end of it (*70 A.D.*) *shall be* with a flood, (*Military invasion*) And till the end of the war desolations are determined. (Daniel 9:26; *emphasis added*)

For more information about the origin of the Antichrist, I highly recommend a book about the Antichrist by Dr. David Reagan entitled, "*The Man of Lawlessness: The Antichrist in the Tribulation.*"[10]

7

The Two Parties of the False Covenant

When it comes to understanding all the details of the false covenant, there are three main proof texts to consider. Daniel 9:27 is one of them, but some prophecy teachers and students don't recognize that Isaiah 28:15 and 18 also provides information about this covenant. In fact, Isaiah was the first to mention this covenant. The Daniel 9:27 and Isaiah 28:15 verses are included in this chapter.

> "Then he (*the Antichrist*) shall confirm a covenant with many for one week; (*consisting of seven years*) But in the middle of the week He shall bring an end to sacrifice and offering. And on the wing of abominations shall be one who makes desolate, Even until the consummation, which is determined, Is poured out on the desolate." (Daniel 9:27; emphasis added)

Daniel 9:27 informs of the following features of the covenant;

- It has a seven-year term,

- It is confirmed by the Antichrist,

- It appears to enable the Jews to reinstate their Temple sacrifices and offerings,

- The Antichrist voids out the covenant in the middle of the seven-year term.

As important as these above details are, they don't explain several important things about the covenant. Fortunately, Isaiah 28:15 give us additional information.

> "Because you (Israel) have said, "We have made a covenant with death, And with Sheol we are in agreement. When the overflowing scourge passes through, It will not come to us, For we have made lies our refuge, And under falsehood we have hidden ourselves."" (Isaiah 28:15; emphasis added)

Isaiah 28:15 provides the following information;

- That the other signatories of the covenant are "Death" and "Sheol,"

- Israel becomes a signatory to avoid an overflowing scourge,

- Israel's participation in the pact involves deceit; "lies" and "falsehood." This suggests that Israel becomes a signatory for politically expedient purposes. These potential purposes are explained later in this book.

•   •   •

> *"Bill, you can't confirm a dentist appointment unless one has already been made. Similarly, the Antichrist can't confirm a seven-year covenant, unless one already exists."*

This is a direct quote from a conversation I had with Bible prophecy expert Jack Kinsella. Jack has since passed on to be with the Lord in March of 2013, but a couple years prior he and I were filming interviews with Jonathan Bernis for the Jewish Voice television show. After the TV shoots, Jack and I had a discussion in my hotel room about the Antichrist's prophesied role in relationship to the false covenant that triggers the Trib-period. That was when Jack made this profound statement to me.

I mention this here to emphasize the important point that the Antichrist merely confirms the false covenant. He may draft up the text of the document and he may even be a party to the treaty, but all the Bible tells us for certain is that he confirms it. This means that something is taking place in the world just prior to the drafting of this document that troubles the Jewish state and warrants Israel's participation in this infamous covenant.

I stated, "*troubles the Jewish state,*" because of what Isaiah says about this covenant. The prophet informs that Israel is concerned about an overflowing scourge that is raging within the world, which has the potential of being harmful to the Jewish state. This concern motivates them to covenant with the party that is perpetrating this overflowing scourge.

What the overflowing scourge might be, when it will occur and who death and Sheol represents, will be discussed later in this book. It is simply introduced here to bring to the reader's attention, that until this scourge sweeps through the world, there is no need for the covenant of Daniel 9:27 to exist.

This is important because all parties to the covenant, Israel, the Antichrist, and death and Sheol, must be present in the world theater prior to the commencement of the Trib-period. When will these parties all be in place? Israel is now and the Antichrist will be swiftly after the Rapture, but when does death and Sheol arrive to implement its scourge campaign? Shortly, I will explain why death and Sheol seem to arrive as the fourth horsemen of the apocalypse. If this is the case, then the false covenant does not get confirmed when the first seal is opened.

Summary About the Timing of the Antichrist's Arrival

The Antichrist will be the first horsemen out of the starting gates after the Rapture. Satan will inject his point man, the Lawless One, onto the world stage the instant he is no longer restrained from doing so. It is conceivable that the Antichrist's arrival on the global stage is during the Post-Rapture / Pre-Tribulation gap period.

Introducing the Antichrist into the global theater as a first order of events is important for Satan because his well calculated plan to perpetrate widespread lawlessness, via deceptive supernatural means, facilitates the Antichrist's ability to become a conqueror. As the choice mediator of the false covenant between Israel, and death and Sheol, the Antichrist must ascend to his position of political prominence without much delay.

Meanwhile as the Antichrist waits to confirm the false covenant, he forms an unholy Church and State alliance with the Harlot. This marriage of convenience becomes politically expedient for him and his Harlot companion. As I point out shortly, the Harlot may be the other covenanting party.

8

The Traditional View of the Seal Judgments of Revelation 6

First Seal: The Conqueror

Revelation 6 - Now I saw when the Lamb opened one of the seals; and I heard one of the four living creatures saying with a voice like thunder, "Come and see." And he said unto me, *"Therefore, when you see the prince who is to come confirm the covenant between Israel and many, as spoken of by Daniel the prophet, then know that the Seventieth Week has begun."* (Rev. 6; *wishful thinking*)

How wonderful would it have been if this is what Revelation 6:1-2 declared! However, nowhere in these two verses is the customary New Testament Greek word for covenant, which is *diathēkē,* even referenced. Yet, these are the very verses where most respected Bible prophecy teachers believe the infamous covenant of Daniel 9:27 gets confirmed and therefore, the seven-year tribulation period begins.

> *"With the breaking of the first seal and the appearance of the first of the horsemen of the apocalypse the dreaded period of time known as the Tribulation begins. This seven-year span of future world history, graphically described in 6:1-19:21, will be the darkest time the world has ever known."* (Dr. Tim LaHaye)[11]

> *"The world yearns for someone to bring peace
> to the Israeli-Palestinian problem. Peace in the
> Middle East is international priority number one.
> According to Daniel 9:27, Antichrist bursts on the
> world stage by forging a peace agreement with Israel
> (See Revelation 6:1-2)."* (Dr. Mark Hitchcock)[12]

Are Dr. Tim LaHaye, Dr. Mark Hitchcock and the many others who hold this view correct? Is this truly and clearly where the book of Revelation places the commencement point of the Trib-period? Maybe, and that's why this chapter is devoted to this traditional view of the details and timing of the Seal Judgments.

The fictitious Revelation 6 quote above could easily have been written this way when compared to an actual quote about a prophecy spoken by Daniel in Matthew 24. Jesus says,

> "Therefore when you see the 'abomination of
> desolation,' spoken of by Daniel the prophet,
> standing in the holy place" (whoever reads, let
> him understand), "then let those who are in Judea
> flee to the mountains.) (Matthew 24:15-16)

Although in the verse above Jesus is addressing an epic event that happens at the midpoint of the Tribulation, it does allude to Daniel 9:27, which says, *"But in the middle of the week He* (The Antichrist) *shall bring an end to sacrifice and offering* (Taking place in the Tribulation Temple). *And on the wing of abominations shall be one who makes desolate,…"*

I make this comparison between the fictional verse, in Revelation 6, to the non-fictional verse, in Matthew 24, to demonstrate how the Bible could have made it perfectly clear that the Seal Judgments of Revelation all fit into the Trib-period. Unfortunately, it didn't.

In general, the traditional view of the seven seal judgments teaches the following:

- The Rapture has occurred and thus, the Church Age has ended.

- The Church is dwelling in heaven when the seal judgments happen on the earth.

- The seals are opened relatively soon, if not instantaneously, after the Church has been raptured.

- The judgments happen in chronological order and in relatively rapid succession.

- Each seal is related to the one that precedes it. For instance, the second seal describes world wars, which results in the widespread famines and pestilences of the third seal.

- The opening of the first seal begins the seven-year Tribulation period.

- All of the seals happen within the Tribulation period. Many believe that the seals happen within the first three and one-half years of the seven-year Tribulation period.

This chapter will generally summarize the seal judgments because several of the following chapters will quote the specific seal judgment verses and explain them in greater detail.

FIRST SEAL – Revelation 6:1-2

"Now I saw when the Lamb, (Jesus Christ), opened one of the seals; and I heard one of the four living creatures saying with a voice like thunder, "Come and see." And I looked, and behold, a white horse. He, (The Antichrist), who sat on it had a bow; and a crown was given to him, and he went out conquering and to conquer." (Revelation 6:1-2)

This is where the White Horseman of the Apocalypse appears. This horseman represents the Antichrist. He is given a bow with no arrows, a crown and then he proceeds forth conquering and to conquer. Below are a couple of quotes that convey the traditional teaching.

> *"The first horse is white, and his rider is given a bow and a crown. Do not confuse this scene with that described in Rev. 19:11, where we see Christ riding in conquest. No, the rider here is Antichrist, the false Christ, beginning his conquest on earth. The fact that he has a bow, but no arrows, indicates that he conquers the nations peacefully. After the church has been raptured, the way will be opened for Antichrist to move in triumph (2 Thess. 2). There will be a false peace temporarily, for he will unite Europe and make his pact with the Jews (1 Thes. 5:2-3)."*
> (Warren Wiersbe)[13]

> *"Revelation 6:1-2. ... John...saw a white horse with a rider holding a bow, wearing a victor's crown (stephanos), and going forth to conquer. Because Christ in His second coming is pictured (19:11) as riding on a white horse, some have taken it that this rider in 6:2 also must refer to Christ, as the white horse...Roman generals after a victory in battle would ride a white horse in triumph with their captives following. The chronology, however, is wrong, as Christ returns to the earth as a conqueror not at the beginning of the Tribulation but at the end of the Tribulation. Also the riders on the other horses obviously relate to destruction and judgment which precede the second coming of Christ by some period of time....A better interpretation is that the conqueror mentioned here is the future world ruler, sometimes referred to as Antichrist though Revelation does not use this term. He is probably the same person as*

the ruler of the people mentioned in Daniel 9:26. This ruler has a bow without an arrow, indicating that the world government which he establishes is accomplished without warfare... The future world government begins with a time of peace but is soon followed by destruction (1 Thes. 5:3). In general, the seals, trumpets, and bowls of divine wrath signal the terrible judgments of God on the world at the end of the Age, climaxing in the second coming of Christ." (Dr. John Walvoord and Roy B. Zuck)[14]

The traditional teaching is that when the Antichrist arrives in Revelation 6:1-2, he fulfills his role as the confirmer of the Daniel 9:27 covenant. Thus, this is when the tribulation period begins, which is also called, Daniel's Seventieth Week. This is also when God's divine wrath that begins to be poured out upon Christ rejecting humanity begins.

The *major premise* behind this teaching is that Daniel's Seventieth Week can't commence until the covenant of Daniel 9:27 gets confirmed by the Antichrist. The *minor premise* is that the covenant can't get confirmed until the first seal judgment gets opened and the Antichrist appears.

This is a logical deduction, but the potential flaw with this reasoning is that nowhere in the descriptions given in the first seal is the covenant of Daniel 9:27 specifically mentioned. Revelation 6:2 alludes to a white horse, a rider, a bow, a crown and the acts of conquering. Perhaps this is where the Antichrist confirms the covenant, but the important question is, does the text of Revelation 6:1-2 specifically state this?

The fact is that it doesn't. If Revelation 6:1-2 is related to the covenant of Daniel 9:27, then why is the only word specifically used for covenant in the New Testament missing? The word is "diathēkē." This word appears 33 times in the New Testament to allude to covenant or covenants.

It is the word used for the Abrahamic Covenant in Luke 1:72, Acts 3:25 and elsewhere. It is the word used for the New Covenant in Matthew 26:28, Mark 14:24, Luke 22:20 and elsewhere.

Diathēkē is the Greek translation of the Hebrew word for covenant, which is "bĕriyth."

Bĕriyth is used 265 times in the Old Testament to identify the Noahic Covenant in Genesis 9:9-17, Abrahamic Covenant in Genesis 15:18 and elsewhere, and every other important related covenant. Most importantly, it is the specific word used for the covenant referenced in Daniel 9:27.

The fact that the only Greek word for covenant is omitted in Revelation 6:1-2 suggests that the traditional teaching is based upon the assumption that the major and minor premises above find application with the first seal judgment. But why does this have to be the conclusion? Why should we assume that this is what the text implies, when it reality it doesn't clearly state this?

Some might suggest the word bow in Revelation 6:2 could be a reference to the covenant. The Greek word used for bow is "toxon." It is only used one time in the entire New Testament in Revelation 6:2. The New American Standard Hebrew and Greek Dictionaries translate the word to mean bow. In this context it appears to be addressing a weapon, like a bow that shoots arrows.

Those who believe this bow could allude to the Daniel 9:27 covenant would direct our attention to the first mention of the word bow in the Bible that appears as a sign of a covenant in Genesis 9:13-16. The first mention of a word in the Bible can be significant. It's called the rule of, or the law of first mention.

> "I do set my bow in the cloud, and it shall be for
> a token of a covenant between me and the earth.
> And it shall come to pass, when I bring a cloud

over the earth, that the bow shall be seen in the
cloud, and I will remember my covenant, which
is between me and you and every living creature
of all flesh; and the waters shall no more become
a flood to destroy all flesh. And the bow shall be
in the cloud; and I will look upon it, that I may
remember the everlasting covenant between God
and every living creature of all flesh that is upon
the earth." (Genesis 9:13-16; ASV)

The problems with connecting the bow of Genesis 9:13-16
with the bow of Revelation 6:2 and the covenant of Daniel 9:27
are as follows:

1. The Genesis 9 bow is a rainbow, not a weapon. Most
   translations interpret the word as "rainbow."
2. The New Testament Greek word of rainbow is *iris,* not *toxon.*
   The Greek word *iris* is found in Revelation 4:3 and 10:1.
3. The Genesis 9 bow is only a token of the covenant, rather
   than the actual covenant.
4. Genesis 9 uses the Hebrew word běriyth to identify the
   covenant, of which the rainbow is merely a token, or
   only a remembrance of the covenant. Běriyth is the same
   Hebrew word that is used for covenant in Daniel 9:27.
   It has already been stated that běriyth is the appropriate
   Hebrew word for the Greek word diathēkē to represent
   the Daniel 9:27 covenant.
5. The rainbow represented a good thing for mankind, but the
   bow in Revelation 6:2 finds association with the career of
   the Antichrist, which is not a good thing for humankind.

It would seem that if the Holy Spirit wanted us to know for
certain that Revelation 6:1-2 is when the covenant of Daniel
9:27 gets confirmed then He would have used the word diathēkē
(covenant), rather than toxon (bow). Or, if he wanted to connect
the rainbow of Genesis 9:13-16 with Revelation 6:1-2, He would
have used the Greek word *iris* instead of *toxon.*

The Second Seal of Revelation 6:3-4 and the Third Seal of Revelation 6:5-6 are explained thoroughly in the next chapter called, *The Alternative View of the Seal Judgments of Revelation 6.* Regardless of whether they start in Tribulation period or in the Post-Rapture / Pre-Tribulation gap period, the interpretations are similar. Below are quotes from The Bible Knowledge Commentary New Testament by John Walvoord and Roy B. Zuck.

> The Second Seal – Revelation 6:3-4. *"With the breaking of the second seal a red horse appeared with a rider empowered to take peace from the earth… In contrast with the first rider who has a bow without an arrow this second rider carried a large sword. This again was a picture of political power with the rider as the world ruler."*

> The Third Seal – Revelation 6:5-6. *"With the opening of the third seal a black horse was revealed with a rider carrying a pair of scales in his hand. At the same time a voice was heard from among the four living creatures saying, A quart of wheat for a day's wages, and three quarts of barley for a day's wages, and do not damage the oil and the wine! "A day's wages" refers to a silver coin, the Roman denarius, worth about 15 cents, which was the normal wage for a worker for an entire day. So this passage is saying that in that food shortage an entire day's work would be required to buy either a quart of wheat or three quarts of barley. If one bought wheat, it would be enough for one good meal; if he bought barley, it would be enough for three good meals but nothing would be left for buying oil or wine. Famine is the inevitable aftermath of war. This will be a major cause of death in the Great Tribulation. The black color of the horse speaks of famine and death."*

The traditional teaching of the fourth and fifth seals differ from the alternative view presented in the next chapter. The fourth seal is quoted below.

> "When He opened the fourth seal, I heard the voice of the fourth living creature saying, "Come and see." So I looked, and behold, a pale horse. And the name of him who sat on it was Death, and Hades followed with him. And power was given to them over a fourth of the earth, to kill with sword, with hunger, with death, and by the beasts of the earth." (Revelation 6:7-8)

The traditional view teaches that this horseman kills a "fourth of the earth." Some believe that this could amount to 1 or 2 billion people. The list of modern day prophecy teachers that believes this is the case includes, Tim LaHaye, Mark Hitchcock, David R. Reagan, Grant R. Jeffrey, Ron Rhodes, Thomas Ice, John Hagee, J. Vernon McGee, Hal Lindsey, Billy Crone and Joel Rosenberg.

Below is another quote from The Bible Knowledge Commentary New Testament.

> *"Here is the aftermath of war, famine, and death. With war and famine people fall prey to a plague and the wild beasts of the earth. The startling fact is revealed that a fourth of the earth, or approximately a billion people by today's population figures, will be killed by these means. It should be obvious that this is not a trivial judgment but a major factor in the Great Tribulation, thus supporting the conclusion that the Great Tribulation has begun. The first four seals may be considered as a unit and a general description of the Great Tribulation as an unprecedented time of trouble."*

The alternative view presented in the next chapter interprets Revelation 6:8 differently. The verse says, *"And power was given to them over a fourth of the earth!!!"* Possessing power and authority over this vast global network of people, the fourth horseman then proceeds, *"to kill with sword, with hunger, with death, and by the beasts of the earth."* It doesn't necessarily mean that they kill a quarter of the earth's population, rather it means they exert control over a quarter of the earth's population.

The Fifth Seal identifies a group of people who have been martyred for their faith. The traditional view teaches that these saved souls became believers after the rapture, but were killed for their faith during the seven-year Tribulation period. The Bible Knowledge Commentary New Testament says,

> *"These are obviously martyrs, mentioned in more detail in Revelation 7. This makes it clear that souls will be saved in the Great Tribulation, but many of them will be martyred."*

The next chapter will point out that these saints of the fifth seal are possibly martyred in the Post-Rapture / Pre-Tribulation gap period rather than the great tribulation period.

The Sixth seal is explained in a later chapter. Both the traditional and alternative views interpret this seal as being opened within the Tribulation period. The sixth seal is clearly when the wrath of God has come. However up to this point in the prior five seals, the wrath of God is not mentioned.

> "...and (men) said to the mountains and rocks, "Fall on us and hide us from the face of Him who sits on the throne and from the wrath of the Lamb! For the great day of His wrath has come, and who is able to stand?" (Revelation 6:16-17; emphasis added)

The Matthew 24 and Revelation 6 Comparisons

The traditional view often connects events in Matthew 24 with seemingly similar events in Revelation 6. This comparison is supposed to evidence that the seal judgments are all part of the Tribulation period. Dr. John Walvoord sums it up below.

> *"There is a remarkable similarity between the progress of* (Revelation) *chapter 6 as a whole and the description given by our Lord of the end of the age in Matthew 24:4-31. In both passages the order is (1) war (Matt. 24:6-7; Rev. 6:3-4), (2) famine (Matt. 24:7; Rev. 6:5-6), (3) death (Matt. 24:7-9; Rev. 6:7-8), (4) martyrdom (Matt. 24:9-10, 16-22; Rev. 6:9-11), (5) the sun darkened, the moon darkened, and the stars falling (Matt. 24:29; Rev. 6:12-14), (6) a time of divine judgment (Matt. 24:32-25:26; Rev. 6:15-17). The general features of Matthew 24 are obviously quite parallel to the events of the book of Revelation beginning in chapter 6."* [15]

Do these prophecies parallel each other and do they clearly evidence that the seal judgments all occur within the Tribulation period? Compare the potential explanations below with a few of these events associated above.

First it's important to note that Matthew 24 seems to identify four distinct sequential end time periods.

1. The birth pangs period of the *Beginning of Sorrows*, (Matthew 24:8). This period precedes the Tribulation period. This period includes the prophecies in Matthew 24:4-8.
2. The *Tribulation Period*, (Matthew 24:9). This period spans the entire Seventieth Week of Daniel. This period includes the predictions in Matthew 24:9-31. Matthew 24:9 would be when the Daniel 9:27 covenant gets confirmed. It is

this confirmation of this covenant that starts the dreaded Tribulation Period. This means that the birth pang events of Matthew 24:4-8 are Pre-Tribulation period events.

3. The *Great Tribulation*, (Matthew 24:20). This period covers the last three and one-half years of Daniel's Seventieth Week. This period includes the events described in Matthew 24:15-31.

4. The *Second Coming*, (Matthew 24:30). This event happens at the end of Daniel's Seventieth Week. This period covers the predictions in Matthew 24:29-31.

The traditional view aligns the wars of Matthew 24:7 with the wars of the second seal in the tribulation period, but there are potential problems with this pointed out below.

> "For nation will rise against nation, and kingdom against kingdom. And there will be famines, pestilences, and earthquakes in various places. All these are the beginning of sorrows." (Matthew 24:7-8)

It's true that the second seal of Revelation 6:3-4 introduces world wars, but some teach that nation came against nation in World Wars 1 and 2. If that's the case, then this prophecy has already been fulfilled in the past and can't be compared to the future wars of the second seal judgment. Also, famines, pestilences and earthquakes are and have been occurring in various places.

Matthew 24:8 identifies a period of birth pangs called the "beginning of sorrows." Is this sorrowful period in the Tribulation period? It seems to precede this tribulation period according to the Matthew 24:9 verse that follows, which says,

> "Then, *after nation comes against nation*, they will deliver you up to tribulation and kill you, and you will be hated by all nations for My name's sake." (Matthew 24:9; emphasis added)

What if World Wars 1 and 2 is when nation came against nation as part of the birth pangs period? If so, then Matthew 24:9 tells us that after these historic wars, "*Then they will deliver you up to tribulation.*" This could imply that the wars, famines and pestilence of Matthew 24:7-8 will have happened prior to the Tribulation period, rather than during it.

Another potential scenario is that nation coming against nation in Matthew 24:7 truly is part of the second seal of Revelation 6:3-4, and the famines and pestilences of that same verse apply to the third seal judgment of Revelation 6:5-6. In these two instances, they would be part of the beginning of sorrows period, rather than the Tribulation period, which doesn't start until Matthew 24:9. This would fit in the alternative view of the seal judgments, which is explained in the next chapter.

In summary, the traditional interpretation of the seal judgments requires us to believe that the Tribulation period begins with the opening of these judgments. This view assumes that the covenant of Daniel 9:27 gets confirmed in Revelation 6:1-2 even though there is no mention of this covenant in those verses.

Furthermore, the traditional view teaches that the wrath of God begins when the seal judgments get opened. However, the first reference to God's wrath is not until the opening of the sixth seal in Revelation 6:12-17.

Although the traditional view could be the correct view, there is an alternative view that deserves an honorable mention. This view is presented non-dogmatically in the next chapter.

9

The Alternative View of the Seal Judgments of Revelation 6

s the Tim LaHaye quote from the prior chapter demonstrated, the traditional view teachers tend to connect the start of the seven-year Tribulation period, a.k.a., (Daniel's 70th week), with the opening of the first seal in Revelation 6:1-2. They believe this Tribulation period starts there and continues throughout Revelation 6:1-19:21.

Although I believe the seven seals conclude within the seven -year Tribulation period, it is possible the first five seals are opened prior, during the Post-Rapture / Pre-Tribulation gap period. This chapter presents an alternative view to the traditional view of the Seal judgments. It explores the details of the first five seal judgments to uncover the clues about their timing.

First Seal: The White Horseman of the Apocalypse

Now I saw when the Lamb opened one of the seals; and I heard one of the four living creatures saying with a voice like thunder, "Come and see." And I looked, and behold, a white horse. He who sat on it had a bow; and a crown was given to him, and he went out conquering and to conquer. (Revelation 6:1-2), (A NEXT Prophecy)

The White Horseman is commonly taught to be the Antichrist. At this point, he can pursue his three-fold career of becoming a political, military and supreme religious leader. The order of events described in these verses are:

1. A white horse with a rider appears.
2. The rider has a bow, but apparently not an accompanying quiver full of arrows.
3. While sitting upon the steed with his bow in hand, he is handed a crown.
4. Equipped with his bow in hand and his crown upon his head, he proceeds to prevail against his enemies; "*he went out conquering and to conquer.*"

The initial question is, does this chronology of events serve as a summary or an introduction to the Antichrist's career? The fact that the seven seal judgments seemingly line up sequentially, each one resulting from the prior one, and the Antichrist goes forth conquering and to conquer his enemies favors the view that this is where the Antichrist gets introduced. The American Standard Version translates that he "*came forth conquering, and to conquer,*" which implies that his actions of conquering, and to conquer are future events from Revelation 6:2 onward.

There are a couple of scriptural anomalies in Revelation 6:1-2 to mention. They are found in the Greek word usage for "bow" and the translations of "conquering and to conquer."

The Bow – The Antichrist's Political Career

The Greek word "toxon" is used for bow. This is the only usage of this word within the entire New Testament. It does appear to be describing a bow associated with archery. During the apostle John's time, this was a primary military weapon, but without arrows it is not effective in winning wars, but it could be used to deter them; *i.e.* a foreign policy based upon national security achieved through the threat of military strength.

Therefore, this bow likely represents the political aspect of the Antichrist's three-fold career, rather than his military role. He possesses a military instrument, but apparently uses skillful diplomacy as part of his rise to political power.

The first phase of the Antichrist's career is his rise to political power. As a rapidly rising world leader he utilizes his position to align himself with the coming global religion of the Harlot. This is one of the first things he does when he emerges on the world stage. Revelation 17:3 says he sits underneath the Harlot and Rev. 17:7 says that from that subservient position that he carries this whore of Babylon to her heights of global religious dominance.

Additionally, this political persona, at some point, gains the trust of Israel and the "many" of Daniel 9:27. This is evident in that they eventually rely on him to mediate between them to confirm the false covenant.

The Conquering – The Antichrist Military Career

The Greek word "*nikaō*" is used in succession in Rev.6:2. The word is used 24 times in the New Testament and it is usually translated as to overcome or overpower. Revelation 6:2 is the only place it is translated as to conquer and most Bible translations interpret it as conquering and to conquer.

Another phase of the Antichrist's career is his rise to military power. As a world leader he is predicted to win major wars. In Daniel 7:24, he subdues three powerful kings and in Daniel 11:40, where he overwhelms the Kings of the South and the North. It appears that when the White Horseman, "came forth conquering, and to conquer," that he is militarily overpowering his enemies.

With the introduction of the Antichrist when the first seal judgment is opened, several important things need to be considered.

1.   *With the introduction of this Lawless One, lawlessness is no longer being restrained.*

2 Thessalonians 2 informs that until the Rapture happens, the Lord protects His believers on earth by hindering the devastating effects of three things. *First*, is Lawlessness, *Second*, is the Lawless One and *Third*, is strong Satanic deception that is empowered through supernatural signs and lying wonders. The fact that the Antichrist is introduced with the opening of the first seal, means that God is no longer hindering these three things.

2.   *The Harlot world religion can form an alliance with the Antichrist.*

Revelation 17:3-7 discloses that the Harlot world religion marries up with the Antichrist in a Church and State union. Once the Antichrist exists on earth, the wedding invitations can go out and this unholy marriage can be consummated.

3.   *One of the required parties involved with the finalization of the false covenant of Isaiah 28:15, 18 and Daniel 9:27 exists on earth.*

The false covenant, which initiates the Trib-period upon its finalization, involves at least three parties. The *confirmer*, who is the Antichrist and the *covenanters*, who are Israel and whoever Death and Sheol represents as the "many" in Daniel 9:27. With the opening of the first seal, at least two of these parties exist on earth. They are Israel and the Antichrist. However, the third party appears to surface subsequently as the fourth horsemen of the apocalypse called, Death and Hades. Hades is the Greek word equivalent for the Hebrew word Sheol.

4.   *The false covenant of Isaiah 28:15, 18 and Daniel 9:27 can now be confirmed.*

The political figure that confirms the false covenant between Israel and the other party is the Antichrist. Now that the White Horseman is revealed, the covenant can be confirmed. This doesn't mean the covenant necessarily exists yet, rather it simply implies that from this point forward, when it does exist, it can be confirmed.

It has already been duly noted that the Greek word *diathēkē*, which is almost exclusively used in the New Testament for the term covenant, is not found anywhere in Revelation 6:1-2. This is one of the reasons why I question if these verses clearly clarify that this is where covenant in Daniel 9:27 gets confirmed.

The other three primary reasons that I wonder if this is where the false covenant gets confirmed are listed below and explained in the interpretations of the fourth and fifth seals that follow.

- The other signatory to the false covenant may be the fourth horsemen of Death and Hades, who likely represent Death and Sheol in Isaiah 28:15 and 18.

- The overflowing scourge that motivates Israel to become a signatory to the false covenant doesn't begin until the fourth horsemen of Death and Hades rides onto the world stage.

- The Fifth Seal saints ask a question that implies that the false covenant has not been confirmed prior to their martyrdom. It would seem that if the false covenant was confirmed prior to their martyrdom period, they would not ask the following question.

"And they cried with a loud voice, saying, "How long, O Lord, holy and true, until You judge and avenge our blood on those who dwell on the earth?"" (Rev. 6:10)

Second Seal: The Fiery Red Horseman of the Apocalypse

> When He opened the second seal, I heard the second living creature saying, "Come and see." Another horse, fiery red, went out. And it was granted to the one who sat on it to take peace from the earth, and that *people* should kill one another; and there was given to him a great sword. (Revelation 6:3-4) (A NEXT Prophecy)

The Fiery Red Horseman represents the unavoidable inevitability that when lawlessness spreads without hindrance throughout the world, peace becomes illusive, world wars occur and global chaos results. In biblical typology, *a great sword* alludes *to great war(s).*

Third Seal: The Black Horseman of the Apocalypse

> When He opened the third seal, I heard the third living creature say, "Come and see." So I looked, and behold, a black horse, and he who sat on it had a pair of scales in his hand. And I heard a voice in the midst of the four living creatures saying, "A quart of wheat for a denarius, and three quarts of barley for a denarius; and do not harm the oil and the wine." (Revelation 6:5-6)

The introduction of the Black Horseman signifies that the darkest of times have fallen upon the earth. When great wars happen, severe suffering results. Famines occur as plagues and pestilences spread uncontrollably throughout the warzones. This creates a humanitarian crisis as refugees' surface and become stranded in the affected areas. The fact that the prior horseman wielded a great sword, implies that the global consequences of the second seal wars were catastrophic.

The third seal imposes the enormous burden upon the international community to resolve the disastrous dilemma before it burgeons out of control. It encourages the expeditious formation of a global government to deal with the escalating emergencies, like world starvation and disease control.

Presently, The Office for the Coordination of Humanitarian Affairs, (OCHA), and The Central Emergency Response Fund, (CERF), are among the United Nations agencies in place to deal with international emergencies. Perhaps they will be the organizations called upon to bring relief to the refugees.

Whatever international agency takes responsibility for administering aid to the afflicted, the Black Horseman instructs them to ration the world's food supplies. The price tag for the necessary food staples to survive becomes fixed at two days' wages. A denarius was the equivalent of a day's wage when this prophecy was written. One denarius will put a quart of wheat inside a family's gallon container and another denarius will fill the remainder of their vessel with three quarts of barley.

The third seal paints a grave picture for the poor, but it's not as distressing for the rich. The horseman concludes his instructions with the command, "*do not harm the oil and the wine.*" This alludes to the luxury items that only the rich will be able to afford. In other words, in the process of rationing the food, do not harm the economic engine that drives the financial recovery, which sustains the existence of the global government.

Fourth Seal: The Pale Horsemen of the Apocalypse

> When He opened the fourth seal, I heard the voice of the fourth living creature saying, "Come and see." So I looked, and behold, a pale horse. And the name of him who sat on it was Death, and Hades followed with him. And power was given to them over a fourth

of the earth, to kill with sword, with hunger, with death, and by the beasts of the earth. (Revelation 6:7-8)

As the seals progress in their chronological order, things go from bad to worse as the world welcomes in the Pale Horsemen of the Apocalypse. I say horsemen, rather than horseman, because unlike its three predecessors the Pale horse has two riders. This sinister tag team rides side saddle in their natural order, Death followed by Hades. Death deals with the material departure of a being from its body and Hades is concerned with the immaterial aspect of a person after death, which is their soul. Presently, when someone dies their soul is delivered to its destination, which is either Heaven if they're saved or Hades if they're not.

Whoever, or whatever their manifestations represent, this diabolical duo seemingly possesses power and authority over a quarter of the world's population to kill people via multiple means. Unlike the second horseman who only had a great sword in his sheath, Death and Hades have a lethal arsenal that enables them *to kill with sword, with hunger, with death, and by the beasts of the earth.*

The traditional teaching is that Death and Hades kill a fourth of mankind, but that's not necessarily what's being said here. Compare the differences in language between the fourth seal and the sixth trumpet in the book of Revelation.

> "By these three *plagues (of the sixth trumpet)* a third of mankind was killed—by the fire and the smoke and the brimstone which came out of their mouths." (Rev. 9:18 NKJV; emphasis added)

This above verse clearly states that *a third of mankind was killed* by the three plagues that followed the sounding of the sixth trumpet. However, Revelation 6:8 says that, "And *power* was given to them *over a fourth of the earth, to kill* with sword, with hunger, with death, and by the beasts of the earth." The New American Standard Bible translates this verse to read, *"Authority was given to them over a fourth of the earth, to kill with sword and with famine and with pestilence and by the wild beasts of the earth."*

Let's unpack this further. *Authority was given to them over a fourth of the earth…*

At a time when the world is experiencing strong satanic deception and is recovering from devastating wars, severe famines and enormous economic scarcities, Death and Hades rides onto the scene. It appears that these two riders come to the rescue and harness global control over one-fourth of the world's surviving population. In the prior chapter, I quoted John Walvoord who estimated that could be about 1 billion people and Billy Crone suggested up to 2 Billion.

If Death and Hades are called to restore order amidst the global chaos, then a global reach of 1 billion people would seem adequate to enable them to execute their campaign successfully. It is likely that some of the other 3 billion, (three-fourths of the earth), survivors are suffering from the consequences of the wars and famines. Perhaps Death and Hades commands their global network of about 1 billion to remedy the dire conditions occurring throughout the world.

However, for the benefits for receiving assistance from the global network of Death and Hades, the needy must follow their dictates. Those who dissent are put to death by either, *"the sword and with famine and with pestilence and by the wild beasts of the earth."*

It may mean that Death and Hades kill a fourth of the earth's population, which is what the traditional view teaches, but more than likely it implies that a quarter of the world's population are faithful followers of Death and Hades. These are devotees so committed to their cause that they are willing to kill their opposition. The fact that Hades takes a lead role in this massive operation infers that this involves a global religious crusade. This future scenario appears to be reminiscent of the historical inquisition periods when the Catholic Church was martyring the so-called Protestant heretics centuries ago.

Isaiah 28:15 and 18 inform us that "Death and Sheol" represent the "many" of Daniel 9:27. They are the other signatory of the false covenant. With the arrival of Death and Hades, (the Greek word for the Hebrew word Sheol), in the fourth seal judgment, it appears that all of the parties of the false covenant are now on the earth.

℘

The alternative view to the timing of the opening of the seal judgments will continue to be explored in several of the chapters that follow. These chapters are mostly devoted to the details of the fourth and fifth seal judgments. They will attempt to put a face on Death and Hades and explain the plight of the fifth seal saints.

℘

10

Do Death and Hades Represent the Harlot World Religion?

"Death slays the body while Hades swallows up the soul" Charles Swindoll[16]

Hades, which is translated as Hell in the King James Version, is the abode of the departed souls of unbelievers. Death and Hades appear together five times in the New Testament Scriptures. Below is a summary interpretation of their usages.

Death is likened to a lethal sting that kills its victim. If the deceased is an unsaved soul, the being goes to Hades, who in turn claims victory over that persons departed spirit, (1 Corinthians 15:55). In other words, Death detaches the soul from its body and then Hades imprisons it.

Christ, having His soul depart from His body after being stung by the death of His crucifixion, conquered Hades through the superior power of His resurrection. In His victory over Death and Hades, Christ now possesses the keys to their gates. This claim is made in Revelation 1:18, which says, "I am He who lives, and was dead, and behold, I am alive forevermore. Amen. And I have the keys of Hades and of Death."

As the gatekeeper, Christ determines who enters Hades and who doesn't. Upon death, a saved soul is locked out of Hades, but when an unsaved soul dies, it enters into Hades and the doors are sealed shut behind it.

As per Luke 16:19-31, Hades is an actual place and it is filled with unbearable torments. In order to avoid being locked into Hades, a person needs to accept Christ as their Savior, after which the gates of Hades can no longer prevail against it according to Matthew 16:18.

Revelation 1:18 is the only verse where Hades appears ahead of Death when they are paired together in scripture. When Death precedes Hades in scripture, it alludes to the death of the body, which is the first death. However, when Death follows Hades, it alludes to the second death pertaining to the eternal separation of the soul from God its maker. When Christ claims to have the keys of Hades and (then also) of Death, He is boldly declaring sovereign authority over the eternal destiny of each and every individual soul.

> "And do not fear those who kill the body, (Death), but cannot kill the soul, (Hades). But rather fear Him, (Jesus Christ), who is able to destroy both soul and body in hell." (Matthew 10:28; emphasis added)

Death and Hades are frightful, but a believer need not be fearful because they are unable to destroy either their soul or body in hell. These are words of comfort, especially to those that will be martyred by Death and Hades as the fourth horsemen of the apocalypse.

Lastly, Death and Hades make their final appearance during the White Throne judgment proceedings at the end of the millennial reign of Jesus Christ. After which, they and all the unsaved souls they had previously killed and incarcerated, are cast into the Lake of Fire.

"Then I saw a great white throne and Him who sat on it, from whose face the earth and the heaven fled away. And there was found no place for them. And I saw the dead, small and great, standing before God, and books were opened. And another book was opened, which is the Book of Life. And the dead were judged according to their works, by the things which were written in the books. The sea gave up the dead who were in it, and Death and Hades delivered up the dead who were in them. And they were judged, each one according to his works. Then Death and Hades were cast into the lake of fire. This is the second death. And anyone not found written in the Book of Life was cast into the lake of fire." (Revelation 20:11-15)

Death and Hades will face the second death, but beforehand as the fourth horsemen of Revelation 6:7-8, they exert power and authority over a worldwide system. Due to the special interests of Hades in the souls of unbelievers, it can be assumed that this global system is spiritual in nature. This massive institution that is apparently comprised of a quarter of the earth's population, becomes a likely candidate for the Harlot world religion of Revelation 17. Revelation 17:6 tells us that the Harlot world religion will be killing believers. The verse says that this woman is "drunk with the blood of the saints and the blood of the martyrs of Jesus."

Who is the Woman Drunk with the Blood of the Saints and the Martyrs of Jesus?

Below are some quotes from respected sources concerning the violent nature of the coming Harlot world religion.

"Those who do come to Christ will be subject to her persecution, and the woman is described as "drunk with the blood of the saints" (Rev. 17:6). The

> *apostate church has been* (past tense) *unsparing in its persecution of those who have a true faith in Christ. Those who come to Christ in the end time will have the double problem of avoiding martyrdom at the hands of the political rulers and at the hands of the apostate church.*" (John Walvoord).[17]

John Walvoord, the former president of Dallas Theological Seminary from 1952 to 1986, connects the Harlot with the apostate church. He says, that as per Revelation 17:6, true believers have faced "*unsparing*" persecution from the apostate church in the past and that this process gets repeated in the future. Tim LaHaye's quote below also emphasizes the future persecution and potential martyrdom of believers at the hands of the Harlot of Revelation 17.

> "*In Revelation 13 we saw that the beast and the false prophet come on the scene in the midst of the Tribulation Period, seeking to make men worship anti-Christ. The complete tyranny of the Tribulation Period is seen in the fact that during the first three and one-half years the ecumenical church of Revelation 17 is so powerful she dominates anti-Christ and kills all believers who refuse to participate with her. During the second half of the Tribulation Period it will be antichrist and the false prophet who kill those that refuse to worship his image and receive his mark.*"[18]

Tim LaHaye acknowledged that during the first three and one-half years of the Trib-period, that Harlot holds a superior role to the Antichrist. Revelation 17:3 pictures the Harlot sitting on the Antichrist and Rev. 17:7 says that the Antichrist carries her during this process.

So, who is the ecumenical church of Revelation 17 according to Tim LaHaye who, "*dominates anti-Christ and kills all believers who refuse to participate with her?*"

In the following quote from his book entitled, Revelation Unveiled, LaHaye qualifies who he believes will be the "ecumenical church." LaHaye says that world religions will form, *"under Rome's headship."*

> *"I can only conclude that Rome is not the only form of Babylonian mysticism, but merely the one that has infiltrated Christianity. And after the Rapture, their leaders that remain will bring all the Babylonian- based religions together with one global idolatrous religion. She may be the one leading all forms of religions at the end time. We are living in a day of ecumenical propaganda calling on the churches of the world to amalgamate... As we approach the end of the Church Age, we can expect to see liberal Protestantism, in the form of the National Council of Churches and the World Council of Churches, being swallowed up by the Church of Rome. This unity movement should not, however, be limited to apostate Christianity. We can expect to see it move toward amalgamating all the religions of the world under Rome's headship because our text states that the religious system at the end time will be a one- world religion. "Where the prostitutes sits, are peoples, multitudes, nations and languages"(Revelation 17:15). This can only mean a one -world religious system."[19]*

The next two quotes also connect Roman Catholicism with the harlot religion.

> *"The meaning here (Revelation 17:6) is, that the persecuting power referred to had shed the blood of the saints; and that, in its fury, it had, as it were, drunk the blood of the slain, and had become, by drinking that blood, intoxicated and infuriated. No one need say how applicable this has been to the*

papacy (Roman Catholicism) … *Let the blood shed in the valleys of Piedmont; the blood shed in the Low Countries by the Duke of Alva; the blood shed on Bartholomew's day; and the blood shed in the Inquisition, testify.*"[20] (American Theologian Albert Barnes - December 1, 1798 – December 24, 1870)

"When the true church is caught up [raptured]*… the Roman Catholic "church" will see a great revival. For a time she has been stripped of the temporal power she once had, but it will be restored to her… And she was drunken with the blood of the Saints and with the blood of the martyrs of Jesus, so that John wondered with a great wonder. Such were her cruel, wicked, Satanic deeds in the past…It could never be true of the literal Babylon. Nor does it mean, as Romish expositors of this book claim, pagan Rome, for if it meant the persecutions under the Roman Emperors, John would not have wondered with a great wonder. And the last page of her* (Roman Catholic Church) *cruel, horrible, persecutions is not yet written. When she comes to power again, she will do the same thing."* (Arno C. Gaebelein) [21]

Why Did the Apostle John Marvel at the Harlot?

"And when I saw her, I (the apostle John) marveled with great amazement." (Rev. 17:6b)

The distinction made above by Arno C. Gaebelein is between *pagan* Rome and *papal* Rome. Pagan Rome alludes to the political Roman Empire during John's time and papal Rome refers to the religious realm that followed a few centuries later.

"Pagan Rome ended and Papal Rome began with the CROSS!! Imperial Rome became PAPAL Rome on October 28, 312 A.D., when

> *Constantine exchanged the eagle for the cross:*
> *And not only so, but he (Constantine) also caused*
> *the sign of the salutary trophy to be impressed on*
> *the very shields of his soldiers; and commanded*
> *that his embattled forces should be preceded in*
> *their march, not by golden eagles, as heretofore,*
> *but only by the standard of the cross.* (Eusebius,
> Life of Constantine, p. 545)."[22]

Arno Gaebelein makes the point that John *"would not have wondered with a great wonder"* from merely witnessing *"the persecutions under the Roman emperors,* (pagan Rome). *"* These persecutions were commonplace during John's time. Gaebelein also explains that for the same reason *"it could never be true of the literal Babylon."*

Some teachers believe the Harlot of Revelation 17 alludes to pagan Rome and there are others who believe that it refers to the literal city of Babylon, Iraq. Gaebelein clearly believed that it was papal Rome, i.e., Roman Catholicism.

The argument could be raised against Gaebelein's statements by saying that John marveled with amazement mostly because he saw the harlot drunk with the martyrs of Jesus in the future. However, contextually it was both distinctly different periods of persecution, the blood of the saints and the martyrs of Jesus, that shocked John. From John's perspective both periods were yet future because papal Rome did not come on the scene until after he died. From our present vantage point, we can suggest that the blood of the Saints period has already transpired during the period of the Catholic inquisitions. Now, the period awaiting final fulfillment is the "martyrs of Jesus."

What John apparently witnessed was two future periods of Christian persecution that would be perpetrated by the same apostate religious system. The system was destined to have a papal affiliation with pagan Rome, and probably why it was given the code name of,

"MYSTERY, BABYLON THE GREAT, THE MOTHER OF HARLOTS AND OF THE ABOMINATIONS OF THE EARTH."
(Revelation 17:5b)

During John's time, Christians would sometimes allude to Rome as Babylon. This was primarily done to avoid political harassment and religious persecution for being Christians. This practice appears in New Testament Scripture. This quote below is from the apostle Peter, who was thought to be in Rome when he issued this greeting.

"She who is in Babylon, (Rome) elect together with you, greets you; and so does Mark my son."
(1 Peter 5:13; emphasis added)

Another example of Christians concealing their faith to avoid Roman persecution was the Christian fish symbol.

"Greeks, Romans, and many other pagans used the fish symbol before Christians. Hence the fish, unlike, say, the cross, attracted little suspicion, making it a perfect secret symbol for persecuted believers. When threatened by Romans in the first centuries after Christ, Christians used the fish mark meeting places and tombs, or to distinguish friends from foes. According to one ancient story, when a Christian met a stranger in the road, the Christian sometimes drew one arc of the simple fish outline in the dirt. If the stranger drew the other arc, both believers knew they were in good company. Current bumper-sticker and business-card uses of the fish hearken back to this practice."[23]

What is the Blood of the Saints?

History demonstrates that the Harlot, if it turns out to be the Catholic Church, has already become drunk with the blood of the saints. All that awaits her final inebriation is to become intoxicated with the future blood of the martyrs of Jesus. Will history repeat itself with the return of the Catholic inquisitions after the Rapture?

Sadly, the Roman Catholic Church was responsible for the death of numerous Christians who held to their true, biblical convictions. Most notable are those who were put to death for refusing to worship the Eucharist. Below are several historical accounts whereby papal Rome was intoxicated from the blood of the saints.

Historical accounts from Foxes Book of Martyrs.

> *"At his trial, [Andrew] Hewet was accused of not believing that the consecrated host was the actual body of Christ. Asked what he truly believed, Hewet replied, "As John Frith believes." "Do you believe it is really the body of Christ, born of the Virgin Mary?" his accusers insisted. "No!" The Catholic bishops smiled at Hewet and the Bishop of London said, "Frith is a heretic, already sentenced to burn. Unless you revoke your opinion, you will burn with him." Hewet said that he would do as Frith did. On July 4, 1533, Andrew Hewet was burned with John Frith."*[24]

• • •

> *"Kerby and Clarke were captured in Ipswich in 1546 and brought before Lord Wentworth and other commissioners for their examination. At that time, they were asked if they believed in transubstantiation. Admitting they did not, both stated their belief that Christ had instituted the Last Supper as a remembrance of His death for the remissions of sins, but there was no actual flesh or blood involved in the sacrament. Kerby was sentenced to burn in Ipswich the next day; Clarke the following Monday in Bury."*[25]

These are just a couple historical examples among many others, which strongly suggest that Roman Catholicism has already fulfilled part one of Revelation 17:6. Papal Rome has already become *"drunk with the blood of the saints."*

It is interesting that one of the primary reasons that believers were martyred by the Catholic Church is because they refused to acknowledge the actual presence of Christ in the Eucharist. Catholics still consider this a grave offense and they take it very seriously.

When the Catholic Church is called upon in the future to serve the revived Roman Empire, as it did in the past, as the official Church of the former Roman Empire, they can be expected to hold fast to their historic doctrines, especially transubstantiation. More Marian apparitions and Eucharistic miracles, which many Catholic leaders still await, will likely be coming in the future as part of the satanic deception in 2 Thessalonians 2. If these supernatural phenomena continue to occur, they will further fuel this religion's quest for greater global control.

Another important thing to consider about the connection between the Catholic Church and the Harlot world religion are the apparitions of Mary. Satan's potential end game for the Marian apparitions is explained in the *Apocalypse Road* book. It is in the commentary of the chapter entitled, "The Queen of Heaven Appears Globally." However, there is one specific apparition to single out in this book.

The Zeitoun account that follows points out that apparitions of Mary are still happening in modernity and will likely resume in the future. If they continue to occur during the reign of the Harlot, they will undoubtedly turn mankind's attention toward the Catholic Church as the global religion.

The Importance of the Zeitoun Marian Apparition

The apparition of Mary in Zeitoun, Egypt occurred between 1968-1970. Millions witnessed this supernatural event, including

Egyptian President Gamal Abdel Nasser. The quote below briefly summarizes what took place.

> *"For more than a year, starting on the eve of Tuesday, April 2, 1968, the Blessed Holy Virgin Saint Mary, Mother of God, appeared in different forms over the domes of the Coptic Orthodox Church named after Her at Zeitoun, Cairo, Egypt. The late Rev. Father Constantine Moussa was the church priest at the time of these apparitions. The apparitions lasted from only a few minutes up to several hours and were sometimes accompanied by luminous heavenly bodies shaped like doves and moving at high speeds. The apparitions were seen by millions of Egyptians and foreigners. Among the witnesses were Orthodox, Catholics, Protestants, Moslems, Jews and non-religious people from all walks of life. The sick were cured and blind persons received their sight, but most importantly large numbers of unbelievers were converted"*[26]

Healings and miracles occurring at an apparition site is not unique to what happened at Zeitoun. In their well- researched book entitled, *"Queen of All, The Marian apparition's plan to unite all religions under the Roman Catholic Church,"* Jim Tetlow, Roger Oakland and Brad Myers state the following,

> *"Numerous healings and miracles have been reported at apparition sites around the globe. In addition, the apparition of the Blessed Virgin Mary has repeatedly announced that her most significant signs and wonders are yet future! She admits that she has not yet revealed her full glory to the world. She predicts heavenly signs and wonders that the whole world will soon witness."*[27]

The Zeitoun apparition occurred within the past century, which supports the possibility the more apparitions will follow in the future. In fact, the quote below from a visionary message predicts that Mary will appear again so that everyone can see her.

> *"I wish to also tell you that before my apparitions end completely, I shall be seen by every denomination and religion throughout this world. I will be seen among all people, not for just a moment, but everyone will have a chance to see me. As I appeared in Zeitoun, I shall appear again so everyone may see me. Pray and help my plans to be realized, not just here, but throughout the world."*[28]

Will Future Apparitions of Mary Facilitate the World Religion of Revelation 17?

Future supernatural apparitions of Mary, like the Zeitoun account, could be the catalyst to the emergence of the Catholic Church as the Harlot world religion. What better way to deceive a world that will be traumatized after the miraculous disappearance of millions of Christians, than to have some supernatural sightings of the Blessed Mother in strategic world locations.

Below are a couple of quotations along these lines. These quotes illustrate what is commonly accepted in some Catholic circles, that more apparitions of Mary are forthcoming.

The first one is from the Marian apparition expert Thomas W. Petrisko.

> *"After the warnings will come the great miracles. Some of these miracles are to be wondrous signs to the world that God exists and that Jesus Christ is Lord. Others will confirm the Virgin Mary's apparitions throughout the world."*[29]

The second quote comes from a visionary message written about by Isabel Bettwy.

> *"At the end of all the apparitions in the world, I* (the Marian apparition) *will leave a great sign in this place and in all those where I have been."*[30]

Consider the likelihood that it would only take one powerful supernatural Mary sighting to garnish the world's undivided attention. One or more timely Post-Rapture apparition(s), along with a reassuring message, could comfort and reconfirm the faith of any Catholics that were left behind.

Remember, Catholics do not believe in a literal Pre-Tribulation Rapture of the Church. It's safe to suggest that left behind Catholics will be susceptible to alternative explanations, especially if they come from their Blessed Mother. All the apparition message has to say, is "That was not the removal of the true Church, rather it was the *yada, yada, yada,* -- or whatever the deceptive explanation might be.

The apparition message might even render a biblical quote like,

> "Soon the wicked will disappear. Though you look for them, they will be gone. The lowly will possess the land and will live in peace and prosperity." (Psalm 37:10, NLT)

> "The righteous will never be removed, But the wicked will not inhabit the earth." (Proverbs 10:30)

> "The Son of Man will send out His angels, and they will gather out of His kingdom all things that offend, and those who practice lawlessness… So it will be at the end of the age. The angels will come forth, separate the wicked from among the just." (Matthew 13:41, 49)

Imagine if the Pope, some Cardinals, Bishops, Priests and other members of the Catholic clergy get left behind. It is doubtful that any of them will want to hear that Christ left them behind.

Most, if not all of them, would prefer to teach that the righteous remained, whereas the wicked were removed from the earth. Moreover, her timely Post-Rapture reappearing would reconfirm their already established beliefs that;

1. Their Queen of Heaven is playing an active lead role within the world,
2. Roman Catholicism is the embodiment of Christ on earth, the "One True Church,"
3. Christ is still present in the Eucharist,
4. There is no Pre-Tribulation Rapture,
5. The Reformation is over,
6. Global peace is finally forthcoming along with the completion of world consecration to the Immaculate Heart of Mary.

Consecration is the action of making or declaring something, typically a church, sacred. This is how Dictionary.com defines the word consecration,

> *"The act of giving the sacramental character to the Eucharistic elements of bread and wine, especially in the Roman Catholic Church."*[31]

The unification of a false world religion after the Rapture will require satanically orchestrated supernatural support. Something spectacular will likely have to occur in order to capture mankind's attention, gain its spiritual trust and persuade it to worship within the harlot system. If Roman Catholicism stays mostly intact and some of its key leaders remain in their places after the Rapture, then this well-established worldwide religious institution could easily be embraced by humanity at large, and the Antichrist, as he begins his nascent rise to political power.

According to Revelation 17:2, this religious system is *"with whom the kings of the earth committed fornication, and the inhabitants of the earth were made drunk with the wine of her fornication."* These idioms express a church and state relationship, through which the masses not only embrace, but become intoxicated by its teachings. Additionally, Revelation 17:15 confirms that the harlot system has a worldwide reach. It says that she presides over "*peoples, multitudes, nations, and tongues.*"

Revelation 17:9 and 18 point out that the religious headquarters of the Harlot is in a "*great city*" that sits on seven hills. At the time these verses were inscribed, Rome was referred to as the city that was built upon seven hills. Below is a quote about this from the Encyclopedia Britannica.

> "*Seven Hills of Rome, group of hills on or about which the ancient city of Rome was built. The original city of Romulus was built upon Palatine Hill (Latin: Mons Palatinus). The other hills are the Capitoline, Quirinal, Viminal, Esquiline, Caelian, and Aventine (known respectively in Latin as the Mons Capitolinus, Mons Quirinalis, Mons Viminalis, Mons Esquilinus, Mons Caelius, and Mons Aventinus).*"[32]

Revelation 17:16, predicts that this system will eventually be desolated by ten kings in order for the Antichrist to introduce his beastly religious system in Revelation 13. This desolation seemingly eliminates the possibility that the harlot system is comprised of an ungoverned interfaith based conglomeration of multiple world religions. Some Bible prophecy experts teach that the Harlot is just that, some sort of a loosely assembled ecumenical cooperative that's religiously tolerant.

There are several problems with this thinking.

1. *How do you desolate all world religions?* How do you eliminate all the snake charmers, witches of Wicca, and New Age mystics, not to mention the far more difficult task of decimating the major world religions of Hinduism, Buddhism and Islam?

Since they are not believers, all of these religious pagans will be left behind. Also, how will all their temples, shrines and mosques become enjoined under one religious' canopy? What single primary city has to be desolated among these religions to make an end of this type of a harlot system? Would it be Muslim Mecca, Saudi Arabia, Hindu Mathura, India or Buddhist Beijing, China? Whichever city, it has to be situated on seven hills and hold the reigns over the harlot system. Revelation 17:18 says that it is the great city that reigns over the kings of the earth.

If Roman Catholicism turns out to be the harlot system, then Rome becomes the target city. If the desolation occurs at Vatican City, then the entire Roman Catholic system becomes disconnected from its head. Additionally, sizeable amounts of the institutions wealth can be easily captured by the Antichrist and the ten kings. This may be a motivator in the minds of some of these ten political leaders.

It's important to note that Mary is the most venerated woman in Catholicism and she is highly regarded within Islam. Additionally, the Hindus worship multiple female goddesses like Lakshmi (goddess of wealth and prosperity), Saraswati (goddess of knowledge and learning) and Parvati (who is the wife of Shiva - the destroyer). The Muslims and Hindus would probably be mesmerized if Marian apparitions followed on the heels of the Rapture.

Moreover, Islam will probably be on a severe downward spiral at the same time because the prophetic wars of Psalm 83 and Ezekiel 38 will have happened, or be about to happen. These wars are discussed in the next chapter. These involve predominately Muslim populations that will be decimated. Should this be the geopolitical scenario at the time the harlot system comes on the scene, then it's doubtful that the Muslim city of Mecca is the city that will be desolated.

2. *A second problem with interfaith view of the Harlot is, how do you convince passive religions to kill true believers in Christ?* Revelation 17:6 says, "I saw the woman, drunk with the blood of the saints and with the blood of the martyrs of Jesus. And when I saw her, I marveled with great amazement."

The apostle uses clear and strong language that depicts a religious system with blood stained hands. It's hard to imagine that a passive Buddhist will embark upon a manhunt to martyr a follower of Jesus. Additionally, whomever the Harlot represents, it must have a history of killing God's saints. The woman is drunk with the blood of two differing groups of believers, the past *saints* and the future *martyrs of Jesus.*

Many religions have no history of killing God's saints. However, the Catholic inquisitions in the 12th and 15th centuries do favor Roman Catholicism as a potential candidate. The Catholics have in the past, stained their hands with the blood of the saints. Interestingly, the prophetess Jezebel, who will be mentioned later in a possible connection with Roman Catholicism, was guilty in 1 Kings 18:5, 13 of killing God's saints in the Old Testament.

Some of you might be thinking that currently the Catholics have turned a new, more religiously tolerant, page from their bloody past. I agree, but when the world is in utter chaos and those who become believers after the Rapture likely speak out against Roman Catholicism, the geo-political environment will be drastically different and much more dangerous. As they did in the past, the Catholics will likely call anyone who denies the actual presence of Christ in the Eucharist a blasphemer. This might be among the reasons that the Harlot is martyring people who become believers in Christ after the Rapture.

For example, J. C. Ryle, writing about the history of the Eucharist from another perspective, explains what happened when people refused to accept the Roman Catholic belief in the Real Presence of Christ within the Eucharist:

> *"The point I refer to is the special reason why our reformers were burned. Great indeed would be our mistake if we supposed that they suffered in the vague charge of refusing submission to the Pope, or desiring to maintain the independence of the Church of England. Nothing of the kind! The principal reason why they were burned was because they refused one of the peculiar doctrines of the Romish church. On that doctrine, in almost every case, hinged their life or death. If they admitted it, they might live, if they refused it, they must die. The doctrine in question was the real presence of the body and blood of Christ in the consecrated elements of bread and wine in the Lord's Supper."[33]*

Revelation 17:6 expresses the utter amazement the apostle John experienced when he glimpsed into the future and witnessed the killings committed by the harlot religion. He says, *"I saw the woman, drunk with the blood of the saints and with the blood of the martyrs of Jesus. And when I saw her, I marveled with great amazement."*

This same apostle John was the one whom Jesus delegated to take care of His mother Mary at the time of the crucifixion. He personally knew the real Mary, the blessed virgin through whose womb the Savior of all men was birthed.

> "Now there stood by the cross of Jesus His mother, and His mother's sister, Mary the *wife* of Clopas, and Mary Magdalene. When Jesus therefore saw His mother, and the disciple (the apostle John) whom He loved standing by, He said to His mother, "Woman, behold your son!" Then He said to the disciple, "Behold your mother!" And

from that hour that disciple (John) took her to his own *home.*" (John 19:25-27; emphasis added)

Concerning the cause of John's amazement, on page 86 of the book by Jim Tetlow, Roger Oakland and Brad Myers entitled, Queen of All, they write,

> "*Why was John shocked when he saw this woman? Who is this woman that would be so terrifying and amazing that John marveled? By this point in Revelation John has been exposed to many horrific events on earth. Why is this the only place he marvels with great amazement ? Dave Hunt, in his book A Woman Rides the Beast, offers some interesting insight into this verse: That a gorgeously clad women should be holding the reins astride such a terrifying, world- devouring beast was just cause for astonishment. John appears, however, to have been dumbfounded by more than that fact- indeed, by the woman herself "when I saw her, I wondered with great admiration{amazement} ." Why? If the women merely represented pagan world religion, John would hardly have been surprised . What could there have been about this woman that astonished him? Had he known her before and was shocked by the unbelievable transformation ?... How had Christ's chaste bride become this brazen whore?*"

Imagine if the Harlot that John is describing in Revelation 17:6 has a connection with Roman Catholicism and the Marian apparitions. The thoughts that would be running through his mind and causing him to marvel with great amazement would presumably be,

> "*Unbelievable, Satan has deceived the Church into believing that the most blessed virgin of the*

Bible has been turned into the bloodiest whore of all whores, the mother of harlots. I was with Mary when she passed on to be in heaven with her son. I wept over her grave. Yet, Satan has deceived people into thinking that she didn't die, but rather was assumed into heaven. Mary should be venerated as the mother of the Savior, but Satan has tarnished her legacy by turning her into a type of Jezebel that kills those who are true followers of the Savior." (Bill Salus)

11

Is Islam the Harlot World Religion?

S ome relatively recent teachers have attempted to connect the fourth horsemen with Islam. They point out that the Greek word "chloros," which is used to identify the pale color of this horse, can also be translated as green. They make the connection with the flag of the prophet Mohammed, which was made of green silk, with this green horse.[34] They further suggest that Mohammed founded Islam in Mecca, Saudi Arabia, which also has a green flag.[35]

More green related topics are found in the Quran, which they believe adds further evidence that the fourth horsemen represent Islam.[36] Another correlation they make is that Islam is a religion of violence and has been responsible for many deaths, and one of the riders on the fourth horse is called "Death."

These arguments are weak and overridden by other prophetic factors, the primary ones that will be explored in this chapter. Also, the Islamic terrorist group called ISIS banners a black flag, but that does not make it the black horseman of the third seal. Similarly, the green flag of Saudi Arabia does not likely represent the pale horsemen of the fourth seal.

Joel Richardson teaches that Islam is the Harlot of Revelation 17 and Mecca is the central city of this world religion. Richardson does not necessarily connect the Harlot religion with the fourth seal judgment. In fact, hardly any Bible prophecy teachers do. Therefore, recognize that connecting

Death and Hades as the fourth horsemen with the coming global religion of the Harlot is mostly being presented in this book as my prophetic hypothesis.

In a debate between he and I in November of 2017, I pointed out the following arguments against his new paradigm shift in thinking on the identity of end time Babylon. These arguments will be listed and then explained below. The debate lasted three hours and has been professionally produced into a well-researched DVD entitled, "The Identity of Mystery Babylon, Mecca or Rome?"

A few of the primary problems I point out on the debate DVD are as follows:

1. After Psalm 83 and Ezekiel 38, Islam will be a religion in decline, which minimizes the potential for Islam to be the Harlot.
2. Islam does not have an exclusive patent on beheadings, which occurs in the Tribulation period according to Revelation 20:4.
3. The Harlot is not the one conducting the beheadings, rather it's the Antichrist.
4. Islam is not historically responsible for the shed blood of two or more of the holy apostles as it relates to Revelation 18:20.
5. The emergence of the Harlot world religion is a future prophetic event and therefore, current world events may not be an accurate indicator of the true identity of who the coming Harlot world religion might be.

After Psalm 83 and Ezekiel 38, Islam will be a religion in decline

Psalm 83 and Ezekiel 38 are distinctly different prophecies. However, the main thing they have in common is that they both involve predominately Muslim countries that invade Israel. They are also the Muslim countries that are located within the heartland of Islam in the Middle East and North and West Africa.

Psalm 83 involves ten populations that are all Muslim and Ezekiel 38 involves nine populations, that with the exception of Russia, are mostly all Muslim. Refer to the maps below for the historic locations and modern identities of these Muslim peoples of today.

Psalm 83 is an ancient prophecy that predicts the conclusion of the Arab-Israeli conflict. It foretells that Israel will defeat their Arab neighbors in an epic war and end the oppression from those peoples once and for all. Ezekiel 38 prophesies that God will stop a massive invasion of Israel supernaturally. Because of both biblical wars, the Jewish state will be emboldened and recognized by the Harlot as a force that must be reckoned with.

Some believe that Psalm 83 and Ezekiel 38 describe the same prophetic event, but they have several distinct differences that makes this highly unlikely. The have;

1. *Different coalitions*, (Psalm 83 involves predominately Arab populations. Ezekiel 38 involves mostly non-Arab peoples). (refer to the maps below).
2. *Different motives*, (Psalm 83 wants to wipe Israel off the map and capture the Promised Land. Ezekiel 38 is to capture plunder and booty from Israel).
3. *Different defeats*, (Psalm 83 is defeated by the IDF. Ezekiel 38 is defeated supernaturally by God).
4. *Different results,* (Psalm 83 ends the ancient Arab hatred of the Jews. Ezekiel 39:7 informs that the Lord makes His holy name known through His people Israel. This was pointed out earlier in the chapter called, *The Next Prophecies of Ezekiel 38-39*).

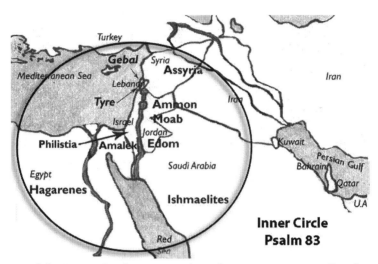

(The Inner Circle map overlays the ancient names of Psalm 83:6-8 over their modern-day counterparts. Note that the Inner Circle is mostly comprised of Arab states and terrorist groups that share common borders with the Jewish state. These ancient civilizations have been Israel's most notorious enemies from time immemorial.)

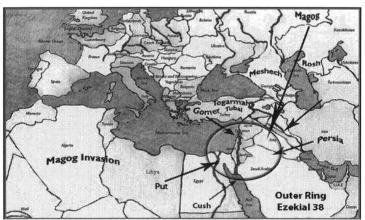

(The Outer Ring map superimposes the historic names of the Ezekiel 38:1-5 coalition over their present equivalents. The arrows depict the location of the coalition members. Note that the Outer Ring of nations does not share common borders with

Israel, include any of the Inner Circle countries or notable terrorist organizations, involve any of Israel's historic enemies, apart from Persia at the time of Esther, or incorporate many Arab states).

Allah loses his Akbar

After these Muslim countries are soundly defeated as a result of these two biblical wars, approximately 600 million Muslims will either be killed, injured, exiled, displaced or become prisoners of war. This will likely cause Muslims throughout the world to question the supremacy of Allah. The argument could be made at that time that Allah has lost his Akbar, which means his greatness. The term Allahu Akbar means "god is great" or, that "Allah is the greatest or greater god."

Moreover, Saudi Arabia becomes adversely affected by these Middle East wars, which mitigate against Mecca becoming the central city of the Harlot. Saudi Arabia is identified in Ezekiel 38:13 as Dedan. In this verse, Dedan appears to be protesting against the Ezekiel 38 invaders, which suggests that Saudi Arabia may play a lesser role in Bible prophecy when the Ezekiel 38 invasion happens.

Islam does not have an exclusive patent on beheadings

> *"Some Christians and ex-Muslims see a direct correlation between Islam and the Book of Revelation about the "end times". It is interesting to note that Revelation 20:4 tells that the faithful Believers in Jesus will be beheaded. One only has to look at militant Islam today to make this correlation. Islam is the only religion that commands this barbaric custom of beheading."[37]* (Joel Richardson)

In the debate DVD, Joel Richardson connects the beheadings that take place in Revelation 20:4 with the blood shed of the Harlot world religion in Revelation 17:6. Although Islam is notorious for beheading people, it does not have an exclusive patent on this as a form of killing people.

In an article called, "The Muslim Antichrist Theory: Joel Richardson," Dr. David Reagan says, "*The point about beheading is flimsy evidence at best. Beheading is not a unique characteristic of Islam. It was one of the stellar characteristics of the French Revolution, and is just the type of horror the Antichrist would institute, regardless of his nationality or religion.*"[38]

There are also interesting articles talking about the potential reinstatement of the guillotine as an effective means of execution. Below are a couple of examples.

- *Maine Gov. Paul LePage: Bring back the guillotine for drug traffickers* – CNN Politics 1/27/16[39]

- *Right-wing French politician Jean-Marie Le Pen wants guillotine reintroduced for terrorists* – International Business Times, 11/21/15[40]

- *'Botched' Oklahoma Execution Proves It's Time to Bring Back the Guillotine* - The Washington Free Beacon[41]
  …Hanging and firing squads would probably be quicker and more painless than lethal injection or the electric chair. But the guillotine really seems to solve everyone's problems…

- *Bring Back the Guillotine* – The Slate, 11/1/13[42]
  …Lethal injection is the wrong way to do capital punishment. Severing the head is the better way to go…

The Harlot is not the one conducting the beheadings

Is it unfathomable to believe that in the future a non-Islamic Antichrist will execute people by the practice of beheadings? Beheadings are quick, effective, painless and better for organ recipients because the bodies of the guillotined prisoners could be more quickly harvested for viable parts.

When it comes to the biblical prediction about beheadings occurring within the Trib-period, the proof text is found in Revelation 20:4. Upon reading this verse below, you will discover that it's virtually impossible to separate the beastly Antichrist from the beheadings. These martyred believers are beheaded in the Tribulation period by the authority of the Antichrist for their refusal to worship him or his image.

> And I saw thrones, and they sat on them, and judgment was committed to them. Then I saw the souls of those *who had been beheaded* for their witness to Jesus and for the word of God, *who had not worshiped the beast or his image*, and had not received his mark on their foreheads or on their hands. (Revelation 20:4; emphasis added)

In Rev. 20:4, beheadings have nothing to do with the Harlot world religion. This is not to say that the Harlot won't incorporate the method of beheadings when she sheds the blood of the martyrs of Jesus in Revelation 17:6, but, the Bible doesn't specifically tell us the method the Harlot employs to execute these martyrs. Therefore, connecting Islam as the religion of the Harlot through beheadings is at best a stretch, and at worst, not even a valid argument.

Islam is not responsible for the shed blood of two or more of the holy apostles

This prophetic requirement is further discussed in a later chapter in this book called, *The Two Judgments of End Times Babylon*. Revelation 18:20 says that the "holy apostles" are avenged when Babylon is destroyed. I asked Joel, "If Babylon represents Islam with a central city of Mecca, then which two or more "holy apostles" were killed by Islam in the city of Mecca?" The answer is none! Islam didn't even exist until centuries after the last apostles of Jesus were martyred. However, two or more apostles were martyred in or nearby Rome. History suggests that they were Peter, Paul and possibly Andrew.

The Emergence of the Harlot world religion is a future event

Lastly, it is important to note that the emergence of the Harlot world religion is a future prophetic event and therefore, current world circumstances may not be an accurate indicator of the true identity of who the coming Harlot world religion might be. This point is brought out several times in the debate DVD.

Joel and I agreed in the debate that the coming global religion of the Harlot is a future event, and yet he continued to connect current trends as potential evidence for Islam as the Harlot's religion. Below are a couple of Joel's quotes from the debate DVD.

> *"I don't want to down play that the prophecy is about the last days. You can look at the verses in Revelation 17:6 and 18:24... The vast majority of all the nations TODAY IN OUR DAY that are killing Protestants, Orthodox, Coptic Christians and Catholics for the name of Jesus they are Muslim majority nations throughout the Middle East. Yet we have still many Protestants TODAY that are saying the real problem is the Catholics. FRANCIS AND HIS GROUPS ARE ABOUT TO START BEHEADING US ALL. Let us open our eyes and look at the biblical descriptions. LET'S LOOK AT WHAT IS UNFOLDING ON THE GROUND..."*

As you can see from these quotes above that Joel Richardson continues to draw attention to what's taking place today, rather than the world's future scenario. He continues with this approach in the quote below.

> *"The point is this. YOU LOOK OUT OF THE EARTH TODAY and as I said all the nations that are the worst persecutors of Christians are all Muslim majority. Now, let me add this. How are the people going to be killed in the last days? It says "I saw the souls of those who were beheaded. So, this is part of Islamic doctrine friends, so this in their Koran, this is part of the history of Muhammad and WE ARE TO BELIEVE THAT ROMAN CATHOLICISM IS GOING TO START BEHEADING US"...*

First of all, this quote connects the beheadings with the Harlot, rather than the Antichrist, which is a point previously pointed out to be problematic as per Rev. 20:4. But why does Joel continue to draw attention to what's happening *"ON THE GROUND"* and on *"THE EARTH TODAY?"*

Apparently, he wants us to focus upon the Islam and Catholic Church of today instead of the future time period that the events of Revelation 17:15 and 17:6 take place. As this book points out, at that future time this world is an entirely different predicament? Another example of his reasoning is observed in the quote below from his book, " Mystery Babylon" on page 136.

> *"While the Roman Catholic Church of history is certainly guilty of shedding the blood of saints, is there any Christian or Jewish blood being shed in Rome today?"⁴³*

In conclusion, Presently, Islam seems like a likely candidate for becoming the Harlot world religion. However, the coming of the Harlot's world religion is a future event. Moreover, if Psalm 83 and Ezekiel 38 happen soon, as some of us suspect could be the case, then Allah will lose his Akbar and Islam will become an unlikely choice for being the whore of Babylon.

12

Death and Hades Kill the Fifth Seal Saints?

Now, it's time to examine who Death and Hades are killing. Understanding who they are martyring helps to answer the following important questions pertaining to them;

1. Who or what do they represent?
2. What is their mission on earth?
3. Why are they killing people, especially believers?
4. What is their role in the overflowing scourge?

Answering these questions will also help to uncover what is the true content of the false covenant and provide some insights as to when the treaty becomes finalized. Let's start by probing into what's taking place promptly after the fourth seal is opened, and some of those important details are provided within the fifth seal.

Fifth Seal: The Martyrs of the Apocalypse

When He opened the fifth seal, I saw under the altar the souls of those who had been slain for the word of God and for the testimony which they held. And they cried with a loud voice, saying, "How long, O Lord, holy and true, until You judge and avenge our blood on those who dwell on the earth?" Then a white robe was given to each of them; and it was said to them that they should rest a little while longer, until both *the*

number of their fellow servants and their brethren,
who would be killed as they *were,* was completed.
(Revelation 6:9-11)

Lo and behold, Death and Hades are killing believers for
professing the word of God and living out their Christian testimony.
True Christian believers may not be the only group they are killing,
but they are at least one of them.

This means that Death and Hades must be perpetrating
a spiritual message that runs contrary to the gospel of Jesus
Christ. The fifth seal saints will hold fast, even to the point of
death, to the biblical narrative, which is that Jesus Christ is the
way, the truth and the life and the only means of salvation as
per John 14:6.

This message of the fifth seal saints must be antithetical to
the teachings of Death and Hades. As such, the quarter of the
world's population that adheres to the religious view presented
by Death and Hades, is called upon to martyr these Christian
dissenters. The slaying of an untold number of Christians implies
that the killing campaign of Death and Hades, is not religiously
tolerant! Apparently, Death and Hades will not be propagating an
ecumenical message, like *"all roads lead to heaven."*

This religious intolerance should terrify the Jews, who at
the same time will be wanting to build the Third Jewish Temple
and reinstate the Mosaic Law. When Death and Hades embark
upon their unholy war against true believers, there will only
be three powerful primary religions left in the world. They are
the religions of the Harlot, Judaism, and biblical Christianity.
Ultimately, there are four religions after the Rapture, but the
fourth, which is the worship of the Antichrist, does not fully
emerge until the Middle of the Trib-period. These four religions
are explained in greater detail in my book entitled, *Apocalypse
Road, Revelation for the Final Generation.*

Some noted Bible commentators believe that the Harlot will be a future apostate ecumenical world church that will embrace all religions except biblical Christianity. They believe this religiously tolerant church with its blending of all religious faiths will be in the war-torn country of Iraq, with a rebuilt Babylon as its central city. Unfortunately, the expositors don't usually explain which one of these religious faiths will arise and lead this ecumenical church. This teaching beckons the question, if Death and Hades represent a tolerant spiritual system, then why are they killing Christians?

13

The Two Killing Crusades that Martyr Christians After the Rapture

U nlike the indiscriminate deaths that will inevitably result from the war(s) of the second seal, there exist two religious systems that discriminately martyr true Christian believers after the Rapture. These two are the Harlot and the Antichrist.

Per Revelation 17:6, the Harlot is *"drunk with the blood of the saints and with the blood of the martyrs of Jesus."* Per Revelation 13:15-17 and 20:4, the Antichrist will kill believers for refusing to receive the "Mark of the Beast."

Unless Death and Hades represents a third campaign of Christian martyrdom after the Rapture, which is not likely, then it must find association with either the Harlot or the Antichrist. It can't be related to the Antichrist for two reasons.

1.   The Antichrist is the White Horseman and Death and Hades are the Pale Horsemen of the Apocalypse. These two horses carry distinctly different riders who operate independent of each other. The Antichrist is given a crown and instructed to go out conquering and to conquer. Death and Hades are given authority over a quarter of the earth's population to kill believers.

2.   The Antichrist's killing crusade doesn't start until the middle of the Trib-period, but Death and Hades and the Harlot world religion begin their targeted murders beforehand.

Therefore, based upon the minor premises above, the major premise is that Death and Hades seemingly finds association with the Harlot world religion. Or, more boldly and directly stated; DEATH AND HADES are associated with "MYSTERY, BABYLON THE GREAT, THE MOTHER OF HARLOTS AND OF THE ABOMINATIONS OF THE EARTH."

If this is the case then whoever THE MOTHER OF HARLOTS represents could be the embodiment of the fourth horsemen of Death and Hades. One possible way to uncover the identity of Death and Hades is to understand how the fifth seal saints become believers.

How Do the Fifth Seal Saints Get Saved?

How do the Fifth Seal Saints get saved? The "white robes" they are given in Rev. 6:11 symbolizes that they are indeed saved. These are committed saints, truly sold out to Christ, even to the point of dying for their faith? Providing they were alive when the Rapture happened, these people were left behind as unbelievers when the miraculous event took place. This means they received Christ as their Savior, after the Rapture.

These saints did not likely learn about Christ from the two witnesses in Revelation 11 or the angel with the everlasting gospel in Rev. 14:6, because the two witnesses and the angel appear during the Trib-period and these saints seem to get saved beforehand. This shocking statement will soon be qualified with an explanation about the timing of the Fifth Seal Saints.

Thus, these martyred saints likely learned about Christ through prior testimonies they had heard, Christian works that have been left behind, and / or by realizing that the Christians were Raptured. This prophetic truth about the Rapture will probably also be echoed by the 144,000 Jewish witnesses of Revelation 7, who will be ministering the gospel of Christ at the time. The 144,000 also get saved after the Rapture.

Here's how the process of conversion might go for the Fifth Seal Saints. After some very basic research, their analytical minds will quickly realize that those who vanished all had *one basic thing in common*; they all believed in Jesus Christ as the Messiah, *i.e.* they were believers. This fact will stick out for some like a sore thumb and be hard for them to deny.

Possessing that understanding, their analytical minds will then logically ask, "Did the Bible have anything to say about Christians vanishing instantly?" They will easily discover the answer is yes, and the event had been predicted about two-thousand years ago, by the Apostle Paul in 1 Thessalonians 4:15-18 and 1 Corinthians 15:50-52.

Their analytical minds will deliberate further and discover that the Bible also says in John 3:16 and 14:6, that "Christ is the way the truth and the life and that God so loved the world that He sent Christ to die for their sins, so that they wouldn't perish but would have everlasting life." This realization will become a motivating factor in their ultimate decision to receive Christ as their Savior to obtain eternal life.

Moreover, after a little more basic study, their analytical minds will become aware that the same Bible predicted that a Harlot world religion and an Antichrist would emerge on the scene after the Rapture. This should cause their analytical minds to turn its attention to the Vatican and seriously question the credibility of the Catholic Church's claims to be the one true Christian church. As this book points out in the chapter entitled, "Why is the Catholic Church Cast into the Great Tribulation?," the Catholic Church remains mostly intact after the Rapture.

The sustained existence of the Catholic Church after the Rapture is a prophecy contained in the letter to the Church of Thyatira. Revelation 2:22 foretells that Thyatira will be going into the Great Tribulation period, which is the second half of the seven-year Trib-period.

The Catholics, represented by Thyatira prophetically, who are left behind will take issue with the Fifth Seal Saints when they question the unscriptural practices and beliefs of Roman Catholicism and its bold claims to be the one true Church. When confronted, some Catholics will likely say something like, "*We are the true church and the removal of many Protestants and Evangelicals brings clarity to this truth. The disappearances of these individuals did not discredit Catholic claims, but to the contrary, proves our standing as the one true Church.*"

The analytical minds of the Fifth Seal Saints will likely respond with, "That doesn't make sense. It beckons the following questions, "*If the Catholic Church is the true Church, and the Bible predicted the unannounced and instantaneous removal of the true Church, then why,*

1. *Is the Catholic Church still on earth?*
2. *Not only on earth, but why is the leadership still chiefly in place and the global infrastructure of Roman Catholicism mostly still intact?*
3. *Also, why did some Catholics disappear, but not all Catholics?*
4. *It seems more realistic to think that Roman Catholicism was a false religion, can you convince me otherwise?*"

Roman Catholicism will undoubtedly have answers for these and many other related questions, but the fact that the Fifth Seal Saints exist clearly evidences that not everyone will be convinced by their explanations.

Roman Catholicism believes that as the true Church, they are the rightful world religion. They believe that they are ordained to consecrate the world to the Immaculate Heart of Mary, with the goal of creating a suitable earthy environment for the Second Coming of Christ. As such, they have no place in their theology for the Rapture. They will dismiss the event by explaining it away somehow.

The disappearances of millions of believers, coupled with the supernatural signs and lying wonders, which will be forwarded by Satan, should strongly reinforce their claims as the rightful one world religion. Believing this is their ordained calling, Catholic leaders will not likely feel the need, nor consider it wise, to be religiously tolerant. With the support of their Blessed Mother, they will carry the torch forward to be Christ's light of the world.

Those who deny the Catholic Church the right to perform what it sincerely believes to be its calling, will put those dissenters at odds with the Catholic Church. They will be marked as blasphemers and martyred as examples!

14

The Three Periods of Post Rapture Christian Martyrdom

Before I officially indict Roman Catholicism as the Harlot World Religion, it's important to discuss the three periods of Christian martyrdom that occurs after the Rapture. The Fifth Seal Saints are the first group, but they are not the only one. This section will also explain why I made the earlier statement that the Fifth Seal Saints seem to get saved before the Trib-period beings.

The two Christian killing crusades, first of the Harlot and second by the Antichrist, take place over the three primary Post-Rapture time periods. They are;

1. The Post-Rapture / Pre-Tribulation gap period,
2. The first half of the Trib-period,
3. The second half of the Trib-period, also referred to as the "Great Tribulation."

These time frames of martyrdom can be determined in part by interpreting the Lord's response to the pleadings of the Fifth Seal Saints.

> "When He opened the fifth seal, I saw under the altar the souls of those who had been slain for the word of God and for the testimony which they

held. And they cried with a loud voice, saying,
"How long, O Lord, holy and true, until You
judge and avenge our blood on those who dwell
on the earth?" (Rev. 6:9-10)

The traditional view of the seal judgments teaches that
these saints of the fifth seal are martyred during the Tribulation
period. Below is the quote from Dr. John Walvoord that is
repeated from a prior chapter concerning the identity of the
saints of the fifth seal.

> *"These are obviously martyrs, mentioned in more
> detail in Revelation 7. This makes it clear that souls
> will be saved in the Great Tribulation, but many of
> them will be martyred.*

The problem I have with this interpretation is found in the
telling question that these martyred saints ask; *"How long, O Lord,
holy and true, until You judge and avenge our blood on those who
dwell on the earth?"*

If these saints of the fifth seal are martyred in the "Great
Tribulation," shouldn't they know how much longer until the Lord
judges and avenges their blood that was shed by the earth dwellers?
Wouldn't they have witnessed the confirmation of the Daniel 9:27
seven-year covenant that starts the Tribulation period? Wouldn't
they be able to accurately identify their existence within the seven-
year timeline? Why would they want to bother the Lord with such
a silly question, and in so doing demonstrate their ignorance of
Bible prophecy? Why would the Lord respond to such a ludicrous
question and devote any portion of the precious pages of the Bible
to state the obvious?

Phase one of the killing spree perpetrated by Death and
Hades is so deadly that these saints cry out with a loud voice
for an answer as to how much longer it will continue. These
saints have already been slain for the word of God and for their

testimonies, but they are obviously concerned for their *"fellow servants"* who are still alive and experiencing this overflowing scourge.

The fact that they don't know how much longer phase one will continue, strongly suggests that they have been martyred during the Post-Rapture / Pre-Tribulation gap period. This period has no specific time attributed to it in the Scriptures.

The timing of the slaying of the Fifth Seal Saints can be logically deduced by realizing that if the seven-year Trib-period had already started, they would be able to calendar the days remaining until the Second Coming of Christ. They don't know how much longer until Christ's return and that's why they ask Him this timing related question?

Other martyred saints, like the innumerable multitude mentioned in Revelation 7:9-17 who come out of the "great tribulation," don't ask this timing question. There is no need because they already know that the great tribulation, which they come out from, only spans the final three and one-half years of the Trib-period. They're not confused about their placement on the prophetic timeline.

However, the setting for the Fifth Seal Saints is different. The situation on earth is so dire, that their timing inquiry can hardly be classified as a naive question. It is doubtful that they ask this question out of prophetic ignorance. They likely realize that the Trib-period only lasts for seven years. I mean, these men and women were slain for the word of God. The fact that the Trib-period lasts for seven years is repeated numerous times in several different ways in the Scriptures. They must know that the Trib-period is coming, they just don't know "how long" until it starts.

It's important to recognize that when the saints of the fifth seal make their decision to accept Christ as their Savior, they will do this knowing full well that it could cost them their lives. Before they are martyred, these saints convert to Christianity at a time in the future when the prophetic awareness is at an all time high. The NOW Prophecies below, will have likely already happened. These saints should not be belittled as ignorant believers who don't know how to monitor the seven-year Tribulation period countdown, and as such, ask how much longer the Tribulation period will continue.

The NOW Prophecies below include, but are not limited to, the following globally impacting events. They are the;

- Disaster in Iran – (Jeremiah 49:34-39),

- Destruction of Damascus – (Isaiah 17, Jer. 49:23-27),

- Toppling of Jordan – (Jer. 49:1-6, Zephaniah 2:8-10, Ezekiel 25:14),

- Terrorization of Egypt – (Isaiah 19:1-18),

- Final Arab-Israeli War- (Psalm 83),

- Decline of America (Ezekiel 38:13), (*America is identified as the young lions of Tarshish*)

- Expansion of Israel – (Obadiah 1:19-20, Jer. 49:2, Zephaniah 2:9, Isaiah 19:18),

- Vanishing of the Christians – (1 Corinthians 15:51-52, 1 Thessalonians 4:15-18).

In addition to the above, the 144,000 witnesses of Revelation 7:1-8 are probably preaching at the time and making it know that they exist in fulfillment of Bible prophecy.

If the traditional view is correct that the fifth seal saints die in the Great Tribulation, I can only think of one reason why these the fifth seal saints would ask how much longer until their blood would be avenged. It would be because they weren't made aware that the Daniel 9:27 covenant had already been confirmed before they were martyred. Perhaps when they are martyred the world is in such a state of disarray that the mainstream media is shut off and the Internet is shut down. This could explain their prophetic ignorance.

The problems with this explanation are below.

1. Daniel 12:4 informs that in the end times knowledge will increase, not decrease.
2. Revelation 11:3-14 says that in the middle of the Tribulation the whole world will watch two witnesses lie dead in a street in Jerusalem. This will require a video technology to be operable worldwide at the time.
3. Revelation 13:5-18 states that no one will be able to buy or sell unless they are registered in the cashless society created by the Antichrist, which gets implemented in the Middle of the Tribulation period. This appears to involve a modern computer technology.

By the way, no matter which timing view you hold on this topic, if the Rapture happens soon, you probably know some of these men and women that will be asking this "how long" question. Undoubtedly, you have important people in your lives that have not accepted Christ yet as their personal Lord and Savior. This puts them at risk of being left behind.

Perhaps you personally haven't made your decision to receive Christ as your Savior. If not, I encourage you to read the appendix entitled, "The Sinner's Salvation Prayer." This appendix will walk you through the process of getting saved. Don't put it off for even another chapter because at any given time you are only one heartbeat away from your eternal destiny.

Back to the question of, *"How long, O Lord, holy and true, until You judge and avenge our blood on those who dwell on the earth?"* Christ's response to their question is interesting. He sums up the metric of time by identifying their Christian condition. Christ says that He will return when the full number of believers who are martyred for their faith is complete. Christ identifies the three phases of Christian martyrdom for them.

> "Then a white robe was given to each of them; (*Group 1*) and it was said to them that they should rest a little while longer, until both the number of "*their fellow servants*" (*Group 2*) and "*their brethren,*" (*Group 3*) who would be killed as they were, was completed." (Rev. 6:11; emphasis added)

The three phases of Christian martyrdom after the Rapture apparently, breakdown in the manner described below.

1. The Post-Rapture / Pre-Tribulation gap period: (*Group 1*) - This phase is when the *Fifth Seal Saints* are slain. It has previously been established in this book, that they are killed by Death and Hades. They are likely among those killed by the Harlot, who is "the woman" in Revelation 17:6, who is "drunk with the blood of the saints and with the blood of the martyrs of Jesus."

2. The first half of the Trib-period: (*Group 2*) - The second phase involves the "*fellow servants*" of the *Fifth Seal Saints*. They are killed during the first half of the Trib-period by the same executioner as the *Fifth Seal Saints*. The Harlot is drunk with their blood also. The fact that they are martyred by the same hands appropriately classifies them as *fellow servants* with the *Fifth Seal Saints*.

3. The second half of the Trib-period: (*Group 3*) - The final phase of martyrdom involves the "*brethren*" of the *fellow servants* who previously died in the second phase. By the time the *brethren* are martyred, the Harlot will have been desolated by the ten kings in Rev. 17:16. This means the *brethren* are killed by a different source. The *brethren* are beheaded by the Antichrist for refusing to worship him

by taking his "Mark of the Beast." The fact that they die during the Trib-period adequately categorizes them with the *fellow servants*, who also died in the Trib-period, as *their brethren.*

The martyrdom that takes place during the killings of groups one and two of the fifth seal saints and their fellow servants will be via the methods below.

> "And power was given to them, (Death and Hades as the Harlot world religion), over a fourth of the earth, to kill with sword, with hunger, with death, and by the beasts of the earth." (Rev. 17:8; emphasis added).

Those martyred in group 3 by the Antichrist will be beheaded for rejecting his "mark of the beast."

> "And I saw thrones, and they sat on them, and judgment was committed to them. Then I saw the souls of those who had been beheaded for their witness to Jesus and for the word of God, who had not worshiped the beast or his image, and had not received his mark on their foreheads or on their hands. And they lived and reigned with Christ for a thousand years." (Rev. 20:4)

15

The Sixth Seal Contains the Wrath of the Lamb

"I looked when He opened the sixth seal, and behold, there was a great earthquake; and the sun became black as sackcloth of hair, and the moon became like blood. And the stars of heaven fell to the earth, as a fig tree drops its late figs when it is shaken by a mighty wind. Then the sky receded as a scroll when it is rolled up, and every mountain and island was moved out of its place. And the kings of the earth, the great men, the rich men, the commanders, the mighty men, every slave and every free man, hid themselves in the caves and in the rocks of the mountains, and said to the mountains and rocks, "Fall on us and hide us from the face of Him who sits on the throne and from the wrath of the Lamb! For the great day of His wrath has come, and who is able to stand?"" (Revelation 6:12-17)

With the opening of the sixth seal judgment it becomes clear that wrath of God has arrived. A great earthquake and cosmic disturbances cause worldwide panic within all of mankind. They will seek places to hide upon the earth because of the widespread devastation.

The traditional view of the seal judgments teaches that the wrath of God begins with the opening of the first seal judgment and continues throughout the executions of the trumpet and bowl judgments. However, technically, there is no other specific mention in Revelation 6 about God's wrath coming upon the earth until the sixth seal judgment.

Whether or not the fifth seal saints are actually martyred during the period of God's wrath could be debated, but regardless, by the time the sixth seal is opened, God's wrath has definitively come upon the earth.

Believers during the Church age are not appointed to God's wrath according to the following verses.

> *Romans 5:8-9* – "But God demonstrates His own love toward us, in that while we were still sinners, Christ died for us. Much more then, having now been justified by His blood, we shall be saved from wrath through Him."

> *1 Thessalonians 1:10* – "…and to wait for His Son from heaven, whom He raised from the dead, even Jesus who delivers us from the wrath to come."

> *1 Thessalonians 5:10* – "For God did not appoint us to wrath, but to obtain salvation through our Lord Jesus Christ,…"

> *Revelation 3*:10 – "Because you have kept My command to persevere, I also will keep you from the hour of trial, (*The Tribulation Period*) which shall come upon the whole world, to test those who dwell on the earth."

> *Luke 1:36* - "Watch therefore, and pray always that you may be counted worthy to escape all

these things, (Related to God's wrath), that will come to pass, and to stand before the Son of Man."

Luke 1:36 tells us that there is a way to escape the wrath of God. The way of escape is the Rapture! The only way to be counted worthy to escape God's wrath is to accept Jesus Christ as your personal Lord and Savior prior to the Rapture event. Do yourself a huge favor, if you haven't accepted Christ as your Savior yet, do it now! DON'T GET LEFT BEHIND!

For further instructions about how to get saved today, read the appendix in this book called, "The Sinner's Salvation Prayer."

In addition to its reference in the sixth seal judgment, God's wrath is alluded to in the trumpet and bowl judgments in the book of Revelation. Below are the following verses dealing with the connection between God's wrath and these judgments.

The sounding of the seventh trumpet, which segues into the outpouring of the seven-bowl judgments, makes it clear that God's wrath is being executed upon the earth.

> "Then *the seventh angel sounded* (His trumpet): And there were loud voices in heaven, saying, "The kingdoms of this world have become the kingdoms of our Lord and of His Christ, and He shall reign forever and ever!" And the twenty-four elders who sat before God on their thrones fell on their faces and worshiped God, saying: "We give You thanks, O Lord God Almighty, The One who is and who was and who is to come, Because You have taken Your great power and reigned. The nations were angry, and *Your wrath has come*, And the time of the dead, that they should be judged, And that You should reward Your servants the prophets and the saints, And

those who fear Your name, small and great, And should destroy those who destroy the earth.'"" (Revelation 11:15-18; emphasis added)

At the conclusion of the seven-bowl judgments the wrath of God is complete.

"Then I saw another sign in heaven, great and marvelous: seven angels having the seven last plagues, for in them the wrath of God is complete." (Revelation 15:1)

The additional related verses to God's wrath in its association to the bowl judgments are, Revelation 15:7, 16:1, and 19.

16

Why is the Catholic Church Cast into the Great Tribulation?

I t's important to start this section by looking at an unfulfilled Bible prophecy that appears to find association with the Catholic Church. The prediction is written in the letter to the Church of Thyatira. The prophetic link between Thyatira and Roman Catholicism is explained in the appendix entitled, "The Seven Letters to the Churches."

> "Notwithstanding I have a few things against thee, (*Roman Catholic Church*), because thou sufferest that woman Jezebel, (*The Queen of Heaven*), which calleth herself a prophetess, to teach and to seduce my servants, (*Catholics*), to commit fornication, and to eat things sacrificed unto idols. And I gave her space to repent of her fornication; and she repented not. Behold, I will cast her, (*the Harlot world religion*), into a bed, and them that commit adultery (*spiritual idolatry*) with her into great tribulation, (*The second half of the Trib-period*), except they repent of their deeds. And I WILL KILL HER CHILDREN WITH DEATH; and all the churches shall know that I am he which searcheth the reins (*minds*) and hearts: and I will give unto every one of you according to your works. (Rev. 2:20-23, KJV; emphasis added)

Hold everything, before I complete the Scripture quote in the letter to Thyatira, let's hit rewind. Did God just say that He "WILL KILL HER CHILDREN WITH DEATH?" These above verses seemingly state that God will kill children of one of the seven churches and that He will do it during the great tribulation, which seems to place these killings during the second half of the seven-year Trib-period.

A commentary by John Gill explains this verse to mean,

> *"And I will kill her children with death,..... Her popes, cardinals, priests, Jesuits, monks, friars, and all that join in the Romish apostasy, they shall be killed with death; there shall be an utter extirpation of them in God's own time;..."*[44]

John Gill, (November 23, 1697-October 14, 1771) was an English Baptist, a biblical scholar and the first major writing Baptist theologian. He says that *"in God's own time,"* that He will kill with death *"all that join in the Romish apostasy,"* including the Catholic hierarchies. I explain shortly that God's own time appears to be during the great tribulation time-period.

This implies that, the Roman Catholic Church, as Thyatira, will still exist on the earth after the Rapture. That's interesting because it's counterpart, the Church of Philadelphia, seemingly ceases to exist after the Rapture. Per Revelation 3:10, Philadelphia is kept from experiencing the seven-year Tribulation period, but Thyatira experiences it in its entirety. If that's not terrible enough, not only do they experience the wrath of God taking place during the great tribulation, but they are going to be purposely afflicted by it!

These verses are addressing the children of Thyatira, which apparently alludes to the faithful followers of Roman Catholicism, rather than literal children. The Bible speaks of the "children of Israel" about 600 times and most of those references refer to the Jewish people in general, rather than singling out their kids.

The question is why? Why would God kill followers of Roman Catholicism with death? Considering that God is a just God, the answer becomes obvious. They are being killed because they have done something deserving of death. In addition to the fact that the institution of the Catholic Church is unsaved, another likely reason that this Church merits being "cast into the sickbed of the great tribulation," and therein be killed, is because it must be guilty of killing God's people.

> *Caveat: I'm not saying that all Catholics are unsaved. This chapter is dealing with the institution of the Roman Catholic Church and not individual Catholics.*

The Greek words used for kill, which is "apokteino," and death, which is "thanatos," can only be translated as to kill or slay someone to the point of their death. They are the same two words used in Rev. 6:8, which says that Death, "thanatos," and Hades have authority over a fourth of the earth to kill, "apokteino," the Fifth Seal Saints of Rev. 6:9-11.

This is not talking about Islam, which has a history of killing God's people, rather this is specifically alluding to the Church of Thyatira. The historic and prophetic connections that justifies this bizarre pronouncement are probably identified in the Catholic inquisitions of the past and in Revelation 17:6 of the future.

The Catholics have a bloody history of killing non-Catholic Christians, who they had identified as heretics. Presently, they are no longer committing these heinous atrocities, but do they deserve no punishment for their bloody past? God is merciful, so perhaps He gives them a pass, but Revelation 17:6 becomes the issue.

I interpret this verse elsewhere in the book, but it says the Harlot is drunk with the blood of the saints AND THE MARTYRS OF JESUS! My concern is that the Catholic inquisitions may repeat themselves again in the future!

I realize that it's hard to imagine that God would kill the precious Catholic Mother Theresa's of the world that are caring for the orphans in India, and I'm not saying that these nuns will volunteer to be on the front lines to slaughter the Fifth Seal Saints with AK 47's. However, if any Catholic gets left behind from the Rapture they are in jeopardy of being cast into the great tribulation and being killed!

During the Catholic Inquisitions, there were nuns who knew that the executions of the so-called heretics were occurring. They didn't necessarily do the slaying, but the fact that they remained faithful to their Catholic faith, rather than excommunicate themselves, made them guilty by association.

Generally, the Christians were sentenced by the Catholic authorities, but then turned over to the secular authorities for their executions. This process might repeat itself. Christian killings will not likely be done by the Catholic hierarchies, rather the martyrs of Jesus could be sentenced by some future Catholic inquisition court and then turned over to the civil authorities for their executions.

For more understanding into this prophecy it's important to pick up where I left off in the letter to Thyatira. The next verse contains some good, but also some dreadful news.

> "But unto you I say, and unto the rest in Thyatira,
> as many as have not this doctrine, and which
> have not known the depths of Satan, as they
> speak; I will put upon you none other burden."
> (Revelation 2:24; KJV, emphasis added)

Let's hit rewind again, what are "the depths of Satan!" This can't be a good thing! How would you like to be a member of a Church that is steeped in Satanic doctrine? This is apparently what the letter to Thyatira says.

Thyatira has allowed Satan to insert terrible false doctrines within Roman Catholicism. One of these erroneous teachings deals with a demonic feminine figure possessing similarities to Jezebel of the Old Testament. The only possible female candidate throughout the entire Church age that comes to mind is the Queen of Heaven, otherwise known as the Blessed Mother, the Virgin Mary, Our Lady of Fatima and many more titles. I compare the striking similarities between Jezebel and the apparition of Mary in the chapter called, "The Two Witnesses."

So, the letter to Thyatira contains some dreadful claims that should severely concern Catholics today. The buzz words and phrases are, "Jezebel," "great tribulation," "kill her children with death" and "depths of Satan."

The Greek words for "*great tribulation*" are, "*megas thlipsis.*" The first tandem use of these words together is in Matthew 24:21, and they identify the timing of prophetic events that happen during the second half of Daniel's 70th week.[45] This is one of the verses that some Bible teachers point to as a proof text for the great tribulation alluding to the latter three and one-half years of the Trib-period.

Concerning the great tribulation and its associated time frame, Dr. David Reagan of Lamb and Lion Ministries says this;

> "*This view is based primarily on a statement Jesus made that is recorded in Matthew 24. According to this passage, Jesus referred to the last half of Daniel's 70th week of years as 'the great tribulation'*" (Matthew 24:21).[46]

Megas thlipsis appears together a total of four times in the New Testament and three of them are associated with events that find fulfillment in the latter half of the Trib-period. These three are found in Matthew 24:21, Rev. 2:22 and Rev. 7:14. The one instance that does not is in Acts 7:11. This verse explains the great suffering associated with the historical famine that came over Egypt and Canaan at the time of Jacob. Most Bible versions translate Acts 7:11 as a great, affliction, suffering or trouble, rather than calling it the "great tribulation."

All four New Testament uses of megas thlipsis deal with specific time-periods. One was in the past, but the three others occur in the future within the second half of the Trib-period. Therefore, the great tribulation mentioned in Rev. 2:22 pertaining to the Church of Thyatira, should not simply be viewed as a period of great suffering that occurs during some undisclosed time-period.

I point out these four usages of megas thlipsis to emphasize that Thyatira apparently enters into the great tribulation period. It's important to compare the translations of Rev. 2:22 provided in the American Standard Version and the New King James Version.

> "Behold, I cast her, (*Thyatira*), into a bed, and them that commit adultery, (*idolatry*), with her into great tribulation, except they repent of her works." (ASV)

> "Indeed I will cast her, (*Thyatira*), into a sickbed, and those who commit adultery, (*idolatry*), with her into great tribulation, unless they repent of their deeds." (NKJV)

These two translations emphasize that Thyatira is cast into great tribulation, like a stowaway might get involuntarily cast off a ship into the sea. Moreover, what better place to punish an adulteress harlot than to confine her to a bed, which is her customary place of business. The NKJV calls it a sickbed, because the great tribulation period is the most sickening of time-periods.

Roman Catholicism became the religious institution that Satan found most suitable to introduce a female type of Jezebel into its theology. This erroneous teaching, which appears to be associated with Mariology, causes the Roman Catholic Church to be cast into the worst three and one-half years ever, which is the "great tribulation" period. Those Catholics who believe in this Jezebel deception, rather than repent of it, will likely be left behind. If they continue to subscribe to this form of idolatry they run the risk of being killed with death during the great tribulation.

How will these killings take place?

How Will God Kill the Children of Thyatira?

This section will explain how God plans on killing the children of Thyatira. There might be multiple means. One of them could understandably be by pouring out His wrath in the great tribulation period, but more than likely, He intends to use the ten prominent political leaders of the end times to fulfill this purpose.

> "And the ten horns which you saw on the beast, these will hate the harlot, make her desolate and naked, eat her flesh and burn her with fire. For GOD HAS PUT IT INTO THEIR HEARTS TO FULFILL HIS PURPOSE, to be of one mind, and to give their kingdom to the beast, until the words of God are fulfilled." (Rev. 17:16-17; emphasis added)

God apparently employs His proven method of the past of using pagan Gentiles to accomplish His greater purposes. The Babylonians were used to discipline the Jews during their seventy years of Babylonian captivity. Then, He empowered the Persians to conquer the Babylonians so that the Jews could return from exile back into Israel. In the instance of the Harlot, He plans on killing her followers through the ten kings.

Will these ten kings only target the Pope, Cardinals, Bishops and Priests, and leave the kind-hearted nuns alone to feed and clothe the poor? Is that a realistic scenario? Or, will the armies executing the commands of their kings ravish and kill these helpless ladies, who happen to be mostly virgins? The verses above say that the Harlot is made desolate and naked, which should concern a Catholic nun dressed in her traditional habit garb at the time.

I apologize for painting a graphic portrayal, but these verses also say that the armies of the ten kings will eat her flesh, and burn her with fire. Burning with fire is reminiscent of the Catholic inquisitions. Many of the martyred Christians at that time were burned at the stake.

The Main Obsessions of the Blessed Mother

The next couple sections of this book explore what the devil has pre-planned for the Post-Rapture future of Roman Catholicism. What is the grander satanic plan that will unfold after the Rapture, when Satan is no longer restrained from performing supernatural signs and lying wonders, during the reign of the Harlot religion?

First, it is important to realize that the apparition of Mary is obsessed with at least five main issues. These must be matters of extreme importance to the Queen of Heaven! They all require her intercession and future intervention, which likely means that Satan's not done with the Virgin Mary.

The Blessed Mother's main obsessions are;

1. Becoming the Co-Redemptrix, Mediatrix and Advocate,
2. Catholics praying the Rosary daily, (The Rosary was personally initiated by this demonic female character centuries ago during one of her apparition appearances).
3. Creating World Peace through her,
4. Consecrating Russia to her Immaculate Heart,
5. The importance of the Eucharist in the salvation process.

Various visionary messages delivered from the apparition of Mary throughout time have often centered upon these topics above. One of my favorites is the apparition's quest to become the

Co-Redemptrix, Mediatrix and Advocate. How convenient is it for Satan to position this imposter of the biblical Mary as a mediator between the Catholic and Christ? If the Devil wants to interfere with a personal relationship between Christ and a potential believer, one great way to accomplish this is to have a demonic intermediator. It has already been established in this book, that the apparition of Mary, as a type of Jezebel, is a creation from the "depths of Satan."

Satan's Plan to Influence Mankind Through the Harlot

> "*In the beginning, there had been one will, the will of God, the Creator. After the rebellion of Lucifer there had been two wills, that of God and the rebel. But now there are billions of wills.*" (Donald Grey Barnhouse, from his book, *The Invisible War*). [47]

This Barnhouse quote illustrates one of the Devil's critical dilemmas, especially when he is no longer hindered by the restrainer of 2 Thessalonians 2:7-12. These 2 Thessalonian verses, which pertain to the end times, inform that Satan plans on employing supernatural signs and lying wonders to deceive people living on the earth. Satan's goal will be to influence the *billions of wills*, representing the mindsets of mankind, to believe in what the Bible refers to as "the Lie."

The Devil's predicament is that God created man as a free moral agent with the ability to exercise his own will and make his own choices. Presently, the Devil exerts a strong influence over the *billions of wills*, but he does not control them.

> "We know that we are of God, and the whole world lies *under the sway (*not the control*) of* the wicked one." (1 John 5:19; emphasis added)

However, when the restraint is removed, it appears that Satan has a clever multi-faceted plan in place to gain greater control over the *billions of wills* within mankind. Signs and lying wonders working in tandem with the existing doctrines, dogmas and catechisms of Roman Catholicism should better align the free wills of man with Satan's diabolical plans, which are to put *billions of wills* into spiritual bondage.

The first phase of Satan's two phased plan to dominate the will of man is the Harlot world religion of Revelation 17. In the second phase the Harlot will be replaced by the religious system of the Antichrist in Revelation 13. These are two differing satanic systems that are custom designed by the Devil to meet his needs for each time-period. The Harlot system prevails during the Post-Rapture / Pre-Tribulation gap period up to the midpoint of the Tribulation period. The Antichrist reign is during the great tribulation period.

During the first phase of the Harlot, lawlessness will abound and misleading supernatural events will make the *billions of wills* who have been left behind susceptible to spiritual deception. Mysterious disappearances of millions of Christians, signs and lying wonders from Satan and generally chaotic world events will present people with uncertain futures. The *billions of unsaved souls* should be more religiously inclined then than they are now. Mostly, people will probably stop denying or questioning the existence of god, rather they will be deciding which one to worship. Satan will employ supernatural deception to influence their decision in favor of the Harlot world religion.

Amidst this backdrop, the Harlot enters in to soothe the sojourning souls seeking a more stable and predictable future. Nothing like a Blessed Mother, with her promises of world peace, to comfort the wearied *billions of wills* that are trying to survive in a war-torn world that is becoming increasingly lawless.

The paranormal will become the new normal and the supernatural will defy the natural and, as such, people's perceptions of reality should be dramatically altered. This becomes further complicated by the defeat of the Gog of Magog invaders in Ezekiel 38-39 via supernatural forces, which could find fulfillment around this time. Israel wins this Mideast war against a massive Russian coalition without hardly firing a shot according to the details in Ezekiel 38:18-39:6.

As temporal existence becomes more threatened, eternal security becomes of greater interest to the *billions of wills*. Salvation of the soul is what the Harlot will offer. So, how does Satan accomplish this through the Harlot world religion?

17

Does Salvation Come Through the Roman Catholic Church?

"*I* *n order to be saved, I (one) must be baptized in the Catholic Church, belong to the One True Church established by Jesus, obey the Ten commandments, receive the Sacraments, pray, do good works and die with no mortal sin on my (their) soul.*"[48]

According to the teachings of Roman Catholicism, salvation can only be obtained through their religious institution via the means that they prescribe. This quote was taken from the book called, *A Catechism for Adults*, which was written by Willam J. Cogan. Father Cogan was a priest and author in the twentieth century, serving the diocese of Chicago. His book, which was published in 1951, received the coveted "Nihil Obstat" and "Imprimatur" around 1958.

"Nihil Obstat," in the Roman Catholic Church, is a certification by an official censor that a book is not objectionable on doctrinal or moral grounds. The "Imprimatur" is an official license by the Roman Catholic Church to print an ecclesiastical or religious book. Thus, the quote above and the ones below from Cogan's book represent the bonafide teachings of Roman Catholicism.

The quotations below are formatted in a question and answer format and are numbered to correspond identically with the related numbers in Cogan's book. Some of the unbiblical answers below illustrate how Roman Catholicism has been, and continues to be used by Satan to put people into spiritual bondage. By comparison, the biblically supported answers to these salvation related quotes are provided in the appendix entitled, "The Sinner's Salvation Prayer."

"Lesson 14

Q-23: *Will I not be saved by accepting Jesus as my personal Saviour?*

A-23: No, I will not be saved merely by accepting Jesus as my personal Saviour or merely by believing in Him. (Cogan answers this question in the first person by using the word "I," which means neither he or anyone else can get saved by merely accepting Christ as their Savior. It requires more than that).

Lesson 16

Q-3: *Has the Catholic Church ever changed its teaching?*

A-3: No, in the 2000 years of its history, the Catholic Church has taught without change the same things taught by Jesus.

Q-4: *Could the Catholic Church ever teach error?*

A-4: No, the Catholic Church could never teach error, because it is the only church which Jesus promised to protect from error.

Q-14: *Can the Pope make an error when teaching?*

A-14: No, the Pope cannot make an error when teaching religion as the head of the whole Catholic Church.

Q-15:   Do all Catholics have to obey the Pope?

A-15:   Yes, all Catholics all over the world have to obey the
Pope because he has the authority of Jesus to rule the
whole Church."

The answers above establish the fact that the Catholic Church
dogmatically teaches that it is the one true church and that the
Pope is infallible. Moreover, the teachings of the Catholic Church
are never wrong and they have not changed over time. Most
importantly, a person can't be saved by simply accepting Jesus
Christ as their Savior, they must also do the things, aka works,
dictated by the Catholic Church.

With those facts established the remainder of the answers to
key questions about Catholic teachings from Cogan's book are
summarized below.

> Lesson 17, A-9: The Catholic Church can never
> be destroyed.
>
> Lesson 10, A-3 to 6: There are two types of sins,
> mortal sins are big sins and venial sins are little
> sins. If someone dies with a mortal sin on their
> soul, they will be sent to hell forever. Mortal sins
> can be forgiven and they include;
>
> 1.   Refusing to accept all of God's teaching,
> 2.   Never praying,
> 3.   Telling serious lies,
> 4.   Not going to Mass on Sundays or Holy Days
>   of Obligation,
> 5.   Getting very drunk,
> 6.   Killing an unborn baby in the womb,
> 7.   All sins of sex,
> 8.   Stealing something expensive.

Lesson 2, A-20: Since attending Mass is essential to avoid going to hell forever, a person must go to Mass every Sunday and on the six Holy Days of Obligation.

Lesson 15: A-17-22: Protestant churches were established by men who broke away from the Catholic Church. There are around 200 Protestant Churches, like Episcopalian, Presbyterian, Baptist, Methodist, Adventist, etc. All Protestant churches are false man-made churches. None of the men who established the Protestant churches had any authority whatsoever to start churches of their own. Everyone has an obligation to obey the Catholic Church because it alone has the authority of Jesus to rule and to teach. To disobey the Catholic Church knowingly is a sin, just as much as disobeying Jesus or His apostles.

Lesson 18: A-3 to 9: It is impossible for a soul to be saved outside of the Catholic Church! It is a serious matter to become a Catholic because, in so doing, a person commits themselves completely and forever under the authority of the Catholic Church. A committed Catholic must always believe everything that the Catholic Church teaches. It is a mortal sin to quit the Catholic Church because it amounts to the rejection of the authority of Jesus Christ.

Need I say more? These teachings compel people to become Catholics and faithfully attend Mass or else they run the genuine risk of going to Hell forever. These doctrinal themes are also included in the Baltimore Catechism, which was the Gold Standard of Catholic education from 1885 to the 1960s. It was commissioned by the Third Council of Bishops in Baltimore.

Below is a quote explaining the Baltimore Catechism from
EWTN.com, which is a global, Catholic Television, Catholic
Radio, and Catholic News Network.

> *"The Catechism with which we, (Catholics) are,
> perhaps, most familiar in pre-Vatican Council days,
> is known as the Baltimore Catechism. This catechism
> was collaborated on by the Bishops of the United
> States in the Third Plenary Council of Baltimore,
> which took place in 1884. It was put together
> and finally issued in 1885 by Cardinal Gibbons
> who, at the time, was the head of the American
> hierarchy. It took the American Bishops from 1829
> to 1885 to put together the Baltimore Catechism,
> which in turn, derived from what was called the
> Roman Catechism or the Catechism of the Council
> of Trent. This document, similar to the Catechism
> of the Catholic Church which came out on June 22,
> 1994, was issued in 1565 by Pope Saint Pius V, and
> was to be the basis of various national catechisms
> and textbooks... The new Catechism of the Catholic
> Church should be read and understood in the light
> of its (the Baltimore Catechism's) history, especially
> Catechesis Tradendae and the General Catechetical
> Directory."*[49]

The quotes below from the Baltimore Catechism reinforce
Cogan's claims and the unchanging teachings of all other
Catechisms in the past and present. At their core, these catechisms
are designed to compel people to become Catholics.

- Lesson Twenty-Ninth: On the Commandments of God.

   #1125 - "It is not enough to belong to the Church in order
   to be saved, but we must also keep the Commandments
   of God and of the Church." [50]

- Lesson Thirty-Fifth: On the First and Second Commandments of the Church.

  #1325 – "The commandments of the Church are also commandments of God, because they are made by His authority, and we are bound under pain of sin to observe them." [51]

  #1327 – "The chief commandments of the Church are six:

    (1) To hear Mass on Sundays and (the six) holy days of obligation.[52]

    (2) To fast and abstain on the days appointed.

    (3) To confess at least once a year.

    (4) To receive the Holy Eucharist during the Easter time.

    (5) To contribute to the support of our pastors.

    (6) Not to marry persons who are not Catholics, or who are related to us within the third degree of kindred, nor privately without witnesses, nor to solemnize marriage at forbidden times."[53]

  #1329 – "It is a mortal sin not to hear Mass on a Sunday or a holyday of obligation, unless we are excused for a serious reason..."[54]

Some Catholics categorize sins in three categories, which are mortal, grave and venial. Mortal and venial sins were previously defined, but what are grave sins? Some ecclesiastical documents, like the Code of Canon Law and the Catechism of the Catholic Church, regularly use the phrase "grave sin" to mean "mortal sin," but are they really the same? What if a sin has been committed that has grave matter but lacks the knowledge and consent needed to make it mortal?

Fortunately, in 1984, Pope John Paul II answered this question once and for all and since, according to Cogan's claims, the Pope can never be wrong, the quote below is the final truth on this matter. The Pope wrote the following,

> "*During the synod assembly some fathers proposed a threefold distinction of sins, classifying them as venial, grave and mortal. This threefold distinction might illustrate the fact that there is a scale of seriousness among grave sins. But it still remains true that the essential and decisive distinction is between sin which destroys charity and sin which does not kill the supernatural life: There is no middle way between life and death.*"[55]

The article from which this quotation was taken goes on to conclude with this statement, "*Hence, in the* (Catholic) *church's doctrine and pastoral action, grave sin is in practice identified with mortal sin.*"

The point made by the Pope is that there is no distinction between mortal and grave sins. There is no middle ground! Mortal sin and grave sin are synonymous. Call the sin that kills supernatural life whatever you want, but if you commit a mortal sin as defined by Roman Catholicism, you go to Hell forever! Eight of these mortal sins, such as aborting a baby, telling serious lies, stealing something expensive and getting very drunk, were previously listed. Have any of you ever committed one of these mortal sins? Per Roman Catholicism, if you have, you are at risk of going to Hell!

At their core, these catechisms and Cogan claims identified in this book are designed to compel people to become Catholics. The explanations below make this conclusion relatively obvious.

1. Roman Catholicism is the One True Church. The Protestant churches are false.
2. Salvation comes primarily through the Catholic Church, rather than merely receiving Jesus Christ as their personal Lord and Savior.
3. People can go to Hell forever if they don't receive forgiveness for their mortal sins in the manner prescribed by the Catholic Church.
4. To be saved a person must,
    a. Become a Catholic
    b. Faithfully partake of the Mass in the acceptable manner defined by the Catholic Church, which is;
        i. Take the Mass every Sunday, and on the days of obligation,
        ii. Perform it inside the Catholic Church,
        iii. Receive the Eucharistic elements by the Catholic Priest.

The plausible way that Satan can gain greater control over the *billions of wills* that have been left behind is to prop up the Catholic Church as the world's One True Church. He can accomplish this by using signs and lying wonders to deceive people, who are already vulnerable to spiritual deception because of the supernatural activities that are occurring in the world at that time.

If people who are left behind from the Rapture don't want to be banished to Hell forever, they need to seek forgiveness through the Catholic Church. The fear of eternal damnation will compel, and the satanic deception will encourage, many people to become Catholics. Even then, their eternity is only as secure as their commitment to the catechisms of the Catholic Church. They will need to take the Mass continually or run the risk of dying with a mortal sin attached to their soul.

This type of spiritual bondage can be easily manipulated by Satan, who has already infused demonic doctrine into Roman Catholicism as per the letter to the Church of Thyatira.

> "Now to you I say, and to the rest in Thyatira, as
> many as do not have this doctrine, who have not
> known the depths of Satan, as they say, I will put
> on you no other burden. (Rev. 2:24)

Stage two of Satan's plan of deception involves the Antichrist.
Since this phase is executed primarily during the Trib-period, the
commentary about this segment will be provided in the next book
of this series, which deals with that seven-year period.

18

The False Covenant of Death in Agreement with Sheol

I n addition to Daniel 9:27, Isaiah 28:15, 18 provides more details about the infamous false covenant. Whatever the true content of this false covenant contains, it is so problematic that it triggers the start of the seven-year Trib-period.

Before interpreting portions of Isaiah 28 in this section, let me caveat that some commentaries believe that the prophecies contained in Isaiah's verses were fulfilled historically with the destruction of the Northern Kingdom of Israel by Assyria in 722 BC. and the Southern Kingdom of Judah by the Babylonians in 586 BC. A few problems with this view are in the following passages:

1. Isaiah 28:5, which addresses the faithful remnant of the Jews. The remnant of Israel is a theme that often finds association with the last days.
2. Isaiah 28:15-18, which informs of;
    a. The ratification and ultimate annulment of the false covenant of Daniel 9:27.
    b. The prior coming of Jesus Christ in typology as the *tried* and *precious cornerstone* of the Temple's *sure foundation*. These verses appear to state that the first coming of Christ had already happened in history. The

coming of Christ happened over 500 years after the destruction of Judah, which nullifies the possibility that all of the prophecies of Isaiah 28 concluded in 586 BC.

3. Isaiah 28:21-22, which declares that the Lord will perform an awesome work. It is an unusual act that involves a *"destruction determined even upon the whole earth."* This judgment happens during the Trib-period when the Lord pours out His wrath on a Christ rejecting planet.

Considering the above qualifiers, this implies that some of the predictions in Isaiah 28 may remain unfulfilled. From that perspective, my interpretation of portions of Isaiah 28 is summarized below.

Isaiah 28:14 forewarns that the leadership of Israel at the time the false covenant is confirmed is a contemptuous group of scornful scoffers. They represent Israel in a condition of power after the wars of Psalm 83 and Ezekiel 38, but in unbelief that Jesus Christ is the Messiah.

Their response to their empowered national condition will not include recognizing Christ, but rather they plan to build their Third Temple and reinstate the Mosaic Law. They believe this is what needs to happen for the betterment of Israel. They will become a signatory to the false covenant to accomplish this. This thinking is pointed out in the verses below. These passages also include God's warning to them about this dangerous national mindset.

"Therefore hear the word of the LORD, you scornful men, Who rule this people who *are* in Jerusalem, Because you have said, "We have made a covenant with death, And with Sheol we are in agreement. When the overflowing scourge passes through, It will not come to us, For we have made lies our refuge, And under falsehood we have hidden ourselves. Therefore thus says the Lord GOD: "Behold, I lay in Zion a stone, (*Jesus Christ*), for a foundation, A tried stone, (*Christ's first coming*), a precious cornerstone, a sure foundation; Whoever believes will not act, (*Concerning the false covenant*), hastily. Also I will make justice the measuring line, And righteousness the plummet; The hail will sweep away the refuge of lies, And the waters will overflow the hiding place." (Isaiah 28:14-17; emphasis added)

Isaiah 28:5-13 had previously explained that by the time the false covenant gets ratified, that the prophets, priests and rulers in Jerusalem were unschooled in the ways of God. The Word of God, which was measured out one precept at a time and was intended to be the guiding principle of their leadership, was not adequately understood by them. Isaiah 28:9 likened their spiritual maturity to that of a baby, "*just weaned from milk*" and "*just drawn from the breasts.*"

Would anyone want a toddler to be the man of their house, let alone rule a thriving nation, especially in the critical last days? Heaven forbid!

Proverbs 25:2 says, "*It is the glory of God to conceal a matter, But the glory of kings is to search out a matter.*" The scornful leadership of Israel at the time they sign the false covenant represents childish infants rather than glorious kings. They haven't thoroughly searched the Holy Scriptures to understand the totality of Gods prophetic word. They likely understand parts of the Old Testament (OT), but not in correlation with their related applications in the New Testament (NT).

Isaiah 28:10 is repeated in Isaiah 28:13 to emphasize that God's word is completed in both portions within the Bible. "Precept upon precept (OT), precept upon precept (NT), Line upon line

(OT), line upon line (NT), Here a little (OT), there a little (NT)."
According to 2 Timothy 3:16, which says that all Scripture is given
by the inspiration of God, that means God's word is purposely
distributed, a *little* in the Old Testament and *a little* in the New
Testament.

Isaiah 28:15 says these deceived leaders are panicked by an
overflowing scourge that is sweeping through the world. In order
to avoid being overtaken by it, they hastily sign a treaty with the
perpetrator of the scourge. God says this is a covenant of death
that is originated from the pits of Hell, (Sheol in this instance).
Concerning Isaiah 28:14-15, Dr. Arnold Fruchtenbaum explains,

> *"In verse 14, God calls the ones making this covenant
> scoffers. Verse 15 gives the reason for this and provides
> God's viewpoint of the covenant itself. It is obvious
> that the leaders of Israel will enter into this covenant
> to obtain some measure of security and to escape the
> overflowing scourge. Hence they will believe that
> entering the covenant will free them from further
> military invasions. However, God declares that this
> is not a covenant of life, but a covenant of death. It
> is not a covenant of heaven, but a covenant of hell."*[56]

Even worse, these scornful leaders of Israel realize that their
underlying motive for covenanting is based upon deceit. Isaiah
28:15 exposes this when it says, *"For we have made lies our refuge,
And under falsehood we have hidden ourselves."*

The motivation for covenanting is not only to avoid the
scourge, but may also include the unrestricted ability to build
the Third Jewish Temple. The Temple could be built before the
false covenant gets confirmed, perhaps after Israel's victory over its
Arab enemies in the Psalm 83 war. However, shortly I will provide
the Scriptural clues that infer that the construction of the Jewish
Temple may be one of Israel's stipulations contained within the
false covenant.

The First Jewish Temple took Solomon twenty years to construct, (1 Kings 9:10). Legend has it that the Second Temple took forty-six years for the Jews to complete, (John 2:20). However, some suggest that the Third Temple could be built in one to two years. [57]

Presently, there are three prevailing points of view about when the Third Jewish Temple should be rebuilt.[58]

a. The Temple will miraculously float down from heaven and settle in its appropriate place.
b. The Messiah will come and facilitate the building of the Temple.
c. The Temple will be built and then the Messiah will come.

The odds are that the Temple will not be floating down from heaven any time soon. Moreover, the Messiah is Jesus Christ and He's not coming back just so the Jews can build their Third Temple. Thus, we can eliminate both of these scenarios. Therefore, the only viable alternative is that the Jews will seek to construct the Temple to hasten the coming of their Messiah, not accepting that He already came over 2000 years ago, in the person of Jesus Christ.

The correlation of the Temple and the coming of Messiah is the important point to the Jews. The coming of the Messiah eventually segues into the establishment of His Messianic Kingdom. The predictions and promises that are destined to find fulfillment during this messianic age epitomize the high point of unfulfilled Old Testament prophecies. The world essentially gets restored to a utopian condition during the Messianic Kingdom.

The probable thinking of the scornful rulers is driven by the belief that whatever it takes to hasten the coming of the Messiah must be done, and without further delay. If it means signing a covenant with a hellish party that's perpetrating a terrible scourge on the earth, then so be it. The means justify the ends because they can accomplish several things through this covenant;

1. Avoid the overflowing scourge,
2. Build the Third Temple,
3. Hasten the coming of the Messiah,
4. End the overflowing scourge, because the Messiah must make an end of it before establishing His benevolent kingdom on earth.
5. Enter into the glorious Messianic Kingdom age.

Isaiah says the covenant is based upon *lies* and *falsehood* and the Jews will believe they have found a *hiding place* by becoming a party to it. However, Isaiah says that like flood waters, the overflowing scourge will come upon them. He warns that their covenant will be short lived.

> "Your covenant with death will be annulled, And your agreement with Sheol will not stand; When the overflowing scourge passes through, Then you will be trampled down by it. As often as it goes out it will take you; For morning by morning it will pass over, And by day and by night; It will be a terror just to understand the report." (Isaiah 28:18-19)

What is the True Content of the False Covenant?

saiah 28:15 and 18 identify two deadly phases of the overflowing scourge, but before I explain what these phases seem to be, I will address what appears to be the true content of the false covenant. Isaiah 28 and Daniel 9 provide several of the contract particulars, but they don't clearly identify the actual content of the false covenant. What exactly is it that Israel and Death and Sheol agree to? Israel is trying to avoid a scourge, but how do Death and Sheol benefit from the deal?

Some Bible prophecy experts believe that the covenant has something to do with resolving the Arab-Israeli conflict. They suspect that the content spells out some acceptable arrangements for a Palestinian state that can harmoniously co-exist alongside a secure Jewish state. Below are the problems with this teaching;

1.   Nowhere in the covenant related scriptures does it say anything about an agreement between the Arabs and the Jews. Isaiah 28:15, 18 says nothing about the Arabs and neither does Daniel 9:27. However, Daniel does say that the one who confirms the false covenant and ultimately makes an end of it comes from the revived Roman Empire.
2.   The Arab-Israeli conflict gets resolved militarily in Psalm 83 and other related verses, rather than diplomatically through a peace plan.
3.   Scriptural clues suggest that the covenant may have something to do with the construction of the Third Temple.

Identified below are some hints that suggest the false covenant has something to do with the construction of the Third Temple.

The first clues are contained in Isaiah 28:16-17. These two verses are sandwiched in between Isaiah 28:15 and 18, which are the verses referring to the false covenant. These passages use terms like a "tried stone," a "precious cornerstone," a "sure foundation," a "measuring line" and a "plummet." These are terms that can find association with constructing a Jewish Temple.

To build the Temple, you start with a *tried stone* that becomes the *precious cornerstone.* This *cornerstone* has a *sure foundation* built around it. The length and width dimensions of a building need to be calculated with a *measuring line,* and the vertical accuracy of a structure is determined with a *plummet,* (plumb-line).

I interpret Isaiah 28:16-17 as a warning to the scornful rulers that drag Israel into being a signatory of this dreadful covenant. These leaders seem to think that they are going to build a Temple and hasten the coming of the Messiah, but Isaiah cautions them not to hastily enter this covenant, because the Messiah has already come as the, *Tried Stone* (1 Peter 2:4-8), *Precious Cornerstone* (Matthew 21:42, Ephesians 2:19-22) and *Sure Foundation* (1 Corinthians 3:11).

The next clue is found in Daniel 9:27, which also serves as a proof text verse in regard to the false covenant.

> "Then he, (*the Antichrist*), shall confirm a covenant with many (*Israel and Death and Sheol*) for one week; (*of seven years*), But in the middle of the week, (*after three and one-half years*) He shall bring an end to sacrifice and offering, (*taking place in the Temple*). And on the wing of abominations shall be one who makes desolate, Even until the consummation, which is determined, Is poured out on the desolate." (Daniel 9:27; emphasis added)

Jesus Christ foretells that this event predicted by Daniel happens in the holy place, which represents the Third Jewish Temple at the time.

> "Therefore when you see the 'abomination of desolation,' spoken of by Daniel the prophet, standing in the holy place" (whoever reads, let him understand), "then let those who are in Judea flee to the mountains." (Matthew 24:15-16)

The intimations in these related verses above, are that by the middle of the Trib-period the Third Jewish Temple will exist. The Antichrist will make a bold statement by entering this Temple and stopping the priestly sacrifice and offering occurring therein. This is in fulfillment of Isaiah 28:18, which says the false covenant will be annulled. What better way to dissolve a covenant than to void out its terms? If the true content of the false covenant allowed the Jews to build their Temple and perform sacrifices and offerings inside of it, then the action taken by the Antichrist to go into the Temple and stop the sacrifice and offering terminates the contract.

A third interesting clue is in the book of Revelation. Several important details are provided in these passages below concerning the benefits to both parties of the covenant. These verses describe what happens in the immediate aftermath of the ratification of the false covenant.

> "Then there was given me a measuring rod like a staff; and someone said, "Get up and measure the temple of God and the altar, and those who worship in it. Leave out the court which is outside the temple and do not measure it, for it has been given to the nations; and they will tread under foot the holy city for forty-two months. And I will grant *authority* to my two witnesses, and they will prophesy for twelve hundred and sixty days, clothed in sackcloth." (Rev. 11:1-3, NASB)

The time frame of "*forty-two months*" is associated with one-half of the seven years of tribulation. The same increment of time is used in the ensuing verse but worded differently as, "*twelve hundred and sixty days.*" It is commonly taught that both usages allude to the first half of the Trib-period.

Thus, the very first thing that appears to happen as part of the implementation of the covenant, is that the Temple gets measured for its construction. The apostle John is given a measuring rod and instructed to measure the temple of God, alluding to the Third Temple. If the covenant called for the construction of the Temple, then this would be one of the first order of events. Measure it so that it can be built.

Some of you might wonder if John is measuring an already existing Temple, but why would he be instructed to do that? That would be an arduous process with the measuring rod he is provided. It would make more sense to simply go to City Hall to get the measurement of an already existing Temple. A building of that magnitude certainly must have its blueprints approved by the city planning commission before it can be constructed. John could get the accurate measurements straight from the blueprints.

Moreover, the measuring process does not take place in the second half of the Trib-period because John, being a Jew and therefore representing the Jews at that future time, would be fleeing from the persecution of the Antichrist, rather than measuring the "temple of God and the altar." In fact, per Matthew 24:15-19, Jesus Christ instructed the Jews to flee from Judea when the Antichrist goes into the temple and commits the abomination of desolation. Jesus did not command the Jews to get a measuring rod to measure the temple of God.

Notwithstanding, the architectural instructions include some restrictions. In other words, the agreement contains some caveats about the building of the Temple that benefit the other covenanting party. The other party are Gentiles who must have some claims to the Temple's outer court and Jerusalem because they are given authority over the outer court, and access to trample through the holy city of Jerusalem. In order for the leaders to build their Temple they will need to negotiate with the Gentiles. This will be a first for them. Historically, the Jews did not negotiate with any Gentiles when they built their first and second temples.

The Greek word used for "Gentiles" in Rev. 11:2 is "*ethnos.*" It used over 150 times in the New Testament and can be translated as Gentiles, nations, pagans or people.[59] The Greek word in that same verse used for "trample," is "*pateo,*" which can also be translated as "tread under foot."[60]

Thus, another possible way to translate this verse is, *the pagans will tread under foot, the holy city of Jerusalem.* They will need this access to make their way to the outer court of the Temple mount, which is given over to these pagan Gentiles. This is an important concession for these pagans. It implies that whoever they are, that they have valid claims to these sacred areas. Presently, the Old City of Jerusalem is divided into four quarters: Christian, Armenian, Jewish and Muslim. The Christian category includes Roman Catholicism.

When the covenant gets confirmed and the Gentiles get awarded access to Jerusalem and authority over the outer court, several Bible prophecies will have likely happened. Two important ones will be Psalm 83 and the Rapture, not necessarily in that order. After Psalm 83, the Muslims will probably lose substantial control over their quarter in the Old City and after the Rapture some Christian and Armenian sections will be vacated by the true believers that resided there. This leaves the Jews and probably a strong Vatican contingency.

It was pointed out earlier in this book that Roman Catholicism appears to remain mostly intact after the Rapture. This does not mean that all Catholics are unsaved, hopefully many of them are born again and will either be Raptured or become true believers afterward. It simply means that the institution of the Catholic Church still exists after the Rapture.

It has also been pointed out that Roman Catholicism represents the Harlot World Religion. Therefore, the pagan Gentiles controlling the outer court and treading Jerusalem under foot are most likely the Catholics, who were not Raptured.

These three clues above seem to suggest that the true content of the false covenant has something to do with the building of the Third Jewish Temple. They also suggest that the covenanting parties are the Jews and the Catholics. But why? Why would the Jews cut a deal with the Catholics? Moreover, why would the Catholics deal with the Jews, especially if they have emerged as the dominant world religion of the Harlot?

The answer would likely be that at the time, Judaism and Roman Catholicism are at loggerheads with each other, and the majority of the Jewish people will be embracing the religion of Judaism, rather than converting to Catholicism.

They will be empowered from their Psalm 83 and Ezekiel 38 victories and on a quest to build their Temple, reinstate the Mosaic Law and hasten the coming of the Messiah. However, they will be troubled by the overflowing scourge that is being perpetrated by the Harlot world religion, which is probably why they come to the negotiating table. The Harlot is killing true Christian believers throughout the world at the time as per Revelation 17:6.

On the flip side, the Vatican will be feeling somewhat invincible because Satan will be propping up Roman Catholicism after the Rapture via supernatural signs and lying wonders. The Vatican will also have the powerful allegiance of the Antichrist and his developing global political infrastructure.

With this global geo-political scenario, probably in place at that time, we can better understand the two phases of the overflowing scourge in Isaiah 28;15, 18.

20

The Two Deadly Phases of the Overflowing Scourge

his is my two cents worth on explaining the two deadly phases of the overflowing scourge. If you haven't read the related preceding chapters, but have just skipped ahead to this part, then you will undoubtedly think I'm crazy after you read this section. So please, consider reading the prior chapters before you read my commentary below.

Phase One of the Overflowing Scourge – Isaiah 28:15

> "Because you have said, "We have made a covenant with death, And with Sheol we are in agreement. When the overflowing scourge passes through, It will not come to us, For we have made lies our refuge, And under falsehood we have hidden ourselves." (Isaiah 28:15)

The first phase of the scourge, *as I interpret it*, is when Israel signs the false covenant with the Harlot world religion so as not to be its next religious victim. The Harlot, represented by Roman Catholicism, is drunk with the blood of the martyrs of Jesus because their biblical narrative is problematic for the advancement of the Harlot's choke hold on humanity.

The Harlot is not religiously tolerant, which sincerely troubles the Jews. They will not buy into her lies, because they are sold out on their own. They practice Judaism and its trappings contained in the sacrificial system of the Mosaic Law. They don't realize that true Christianity is the completion of Judaism. Jesus is the Messiah who already came, but they are in denial about this reality.

> "Therefore the, (Mosaic) law was our tutor *to bring us* to Christ, that we might be justified by faith. But after faith has come, we are no longer under a tutor." (Galatians 3:24-25; emphasis added)

The fact of the matter is that the law was fulfilled by Christ, (Matthew 5:17-18), which rendered it inoperative. Now people are saved by faith through the gift of God's grace, rather than by the works of the law, (Ephesians 2:8-9). Aren't you glad that's how God has now made salvation available to you?

By locking arms with the Harlot, the Jews believe that they can appease her temporarily. They believe that she will not attempt to be drunk with the blood of the martyrs of Jesus and, also the blood of the Jews. The Jews are willing to concede some sacred holy territory by giving the Harlot authority over the outer court and access to tread Jerusalem under foot, because they will be able to build their Temple and hasten the coming of their long-awaited Messiah.

The Jews reason that the means of signing this deceitful covenant justifies the ends of invoking the coming of the Messiah. In their estimation, once the Messiah comes He eliminates the pagan Harlot system. They believe that in the end, it's the Harlot and not them, who gets the short end of the stick in this seven-year covenant.

After the ratification of the covenant the Jews build their Temple and enjoy a temporary period of pseudo peace. They await the imminent coming of their Messiah to destroy the Harlot and usher in His Messianic Kingdom, which is the high point of all Old Testament prophecy.

Phase Two of the Overflowing Scourge – Isaiah 28:18

> "Your covenant with death will be annulled, And your agreement with Sheol will not stand; When the overflowing scourge passes through, Then you will be trampled down by it." (Isaiah 28:18)

However, something goes horribly wrong for the Jews and that's phase two of the overflowing scourge. This is a good place to lay out the likely chronological sequence of events that happen in the middle of the Trib-period. These prophecies set the stage for the second phase of the overflowing scourge.

1. Satan loses a war in heaven, which forces him and his fallen angels to depart from heaven and flee to the earth, (Rev. 12:7-9).
2. Realizing his time is short, (Rev. 12:12), Satan commands his political point man on earth, the Antichrist, to exalt himself above all gods, (Daniel 11:36-37), and to ally with the False Prophet to usurp the religious system of the Antichrist over all others, (Rev. 13:11-17). Thus, the Antichrist needs to do several things, which are;
   a. Form an alliance with ten powerful political leaders, (ten kings), to desolate the Harlot religion, (Rev. 17:16), and replace it with his own religious system,
   b. Personally, go to Jerusalem and kill the Two Witnesses, (Rev. 11:7),
   c. Personally, enter the Third Jewish Temple and make an end of the Jewish sacrifices and offerings, which annuls the false covenant, (Matthew 24:15, Daniel 9:27 and 12:11),
   d. Begin a genocidal campaign of the Jews and in so doing end the religion of Judaism, (Zechariah 13:8),
   e. Force people to worship the Antichrist by taking the "Mark of the Beast," (Rev. 13:14),
   f. Martyr biblical Christians for not taking his beastly mark. (Rev. 13:15, Rev. 20:4).

It is phase two of the scourge that Jesus warned about in Matthew 24:15-22. He instructed the Jews to flee immediately to the mountains, alluding to Petra in Jordan. He issued this command because He wanted to protect the Jews from the final genocide attempt against them, which will be executed by the Antichrist. This was predicted in Zechariah 13:8 with imagery of the scenario provided in Isaiah 28:19-20. A faithful remnant of Jews will emerge in Petra Jordan, and Jesus ultimately comes for them there according to Isaiah 63:1-8.

Summary of the Two Phased Overflowing Scourge

The overflowing scourge has two phases and each phase is carried out by different sources. The perpetrator of phase one is the Harlot world religion and the executioner of phase two is the Antichrist. Both phases involve martyrdom of biblical Christians, but only phase two involves the killing of the Jews.

The irony for the Jews in Isaiah 28:15-18 is that they will trust the Antichrist to confirm the false covenant, but shortly thereafter he will betray their trust by annulling the covenant that he brokered. The warning from the prophet Isaiah in these verses might be restated as follows:

> "Behold you scornful rulers of Jerusalem that become signatories of the false covenant. You are making a grave mistake on behalf of Israel. This devilish deal will bring death upon your people. It has been designed by Satan out from the pits of Hell (Sheol). The political leader you believe will guarantee your national security, will betray you. He will first eliminate the other covenanting party of the Harlot world religion, and then he will commit genocide of the Jews. If you would have searched all the Scriptures thoroughly, you would have understood that Jesus Christ is the Messiah! You would not have acted in haste to sign this covenant with the hopes of hastening the coming of some other messiah. You would have known better!"

21

The Two Witnesses

Revelation 11:3-14 foretells the coming of two powerful witnesses. It is commonly taught that they are active during the first half of the Trib-Period, which would make their arrival into the world theater a NEXT prophecy. The verse below establishes their three and one-half years of ministry on the prophetic calendar. (1260 days ÷ 360 days = 3.5 years).

> 'And I will give power to my two witnesses, and they will prophesy one thousand two hundred and sixty days, clothed in sackcloth." (Rev. 11:3)

Who Are The Two Witnesses?

It is possible, from the clues provided in Revelation 11:3-14, to make an educated guess as to who the Two Witnesses are. Some believe that they are Moses and Elijah. Others suggest they are Elijah and Enoch. Some have posited that they could be none of the above, but might be two entirely new faces.

I don't favor the "new faces" possibility for the following two reasons.

First, Revelation 11:4 says, "*These are the two olive trees and the two lampstands standing before the God of the earth.*" This seems to correlate directly with a vision described in Zechariah 4 of the Old Testament. The same two olive trees show up three times in Zechariah's verses, (Zechariah 4:3,11-12). Referring to the identity of the two olive trees, Zechariah 4:14 says, "So he said, "*These are* the two anointed ones, who stand beside the Lord of the whole earth." If these are the two anointed ones, then it is highly doubtful that they are new faces on the earth in the end times, who serve the Lord for only three and one-half years.

Second, there are clues identified below that support Moses and Elijah are these two witnesses.

1. Moses and Elijah appeared together on the mount of transfiguration. (Matthew 17:3-4). If they appeared together in a significant event of the past, they will likely appear together in the future as well.
2. Moses and Elijah possessed in the past the similar supernatural powers that the Two Witnesses possess in the future. The verses below describe these powers.

> "These are the two olive trees and the two lampstands standing before the God of the earth. And if anyone wants to harm them, *fire* proceeds from their mouth and devours their enemies. And if anyone wants to harm them, he must be killed in this manner. These have power to shut heaven, so that *no rain* falls in the days of their prophecy; and they have power over *waters to turn them to blood*, and to *strike the earth with all plagues*, as often as they desire." (Revelation 11:4-6; emphasis added)

Elijah's former powers concerning *rain* are documented in 1 Kings 17:1, 1 Kings 18:1, 45, James 5:17-18. Elijah also called down *fire* from heaven in 1 Kings 18:38, and 2 Kings 1:10. Moses turned the *waters to blood* in Exodus 7:20-21. Concerning Moses and his ability to strike the earth with all plagues, he struck Egypt with ten plagues, which led to the Exodus of the Hebrews out of Egyptian bondage. The plagues were;[61]

- *First Plague*: Water turned to blood, (Exodus 7:20-21),

- *Second Plague*: Frog infestation throughout Egypt, (Exodus 8:2-4),

- *Third Plague*: Gnats or lice infestation throughout Egypt, (Exodus 8:16-17),

- *Fourth Plague*: Swarms of flies on the people and in their houses, (Exodus 18:21),

- *Fifth Plague*: Livestock diseased, (Exodus 9:3),

- *Sixth Plague*: Boil infections upon the Egyptians, (Exodus 9:8-11),

- *Seventh Plague*: Hailstones rain down upon Egypt, (Exodus 9:18),

- *Eighth Plague*: Locusts cover the face of the earth, (Exodus 10:4-5),

- *Ninth Plague*: Thick blanket of darkness over Egypt, (Exodus 10:21-22),

- *Tenth Plague*: Deaths of the firstborn in Egypt, (Exodus 11:4-5).

It's worthy to note, that some of these plagues seem to be repeated in some variation within some of the trumpet judgments detailed in Revelation 8-9. The first trumpet involves hail and fire mingled with blood (Rev. 8:7). The second trumpet predicts that one-third of the seas will turn into blood (Rev. 8:8). The fourth trumpet says that one-third of the sun, moon and stars become darkened (Rev. 8:12). The fifth trumpet involves a plague of locusts (Rev. 9:3). However, this locust plague is not caused by Moses, but rather it appears to be outsourced by Satan.

It is possible that the trumpet judgments are occurring within the same time-period that the Two Witnesses are ministering on the earth. The two witnesses may not have anything to do with the worldwide plagues caused by the trumpet judgments, but something these two individuals do severely angers most of mankind as per the verses below. People around the world rejoice, rather than grieve, when these two witnesses are killed by the Antichrist in Jerusalem. This suggests that even though they are stationed in Jerusalem, their ministries and powers have a global impact.

> "When they finish their testimony, the beast (Antichrist) that ascends out of the bottomless pit will make war against them, overcome them, and kill them. And their dead bodies *will lie* in the street of the great city which spiritually is called Sodom and Egypt, where also our Lord was crucified. Then *those* from the peoples, tribes, tongues, and nations will see their dead bodies three-and-a-half days, and not allow their dead bodies to be put into graves. And those who dwell on the earth will rejoice over them, make merry, and send gifts to one another, because these two prophets tormented those who dwell on the earth." (Rev. 11:7-10)

More reasons why I favor Moses and Elijah as the Two Witnesses continues below.

3. Elijah was caught up in a whirlwind to heaven and never experienced death, (2 Kings 2:11-12). Enoch was also caught up to heaven, which is why some believe that he could be one of the Two Witnesses, (Genesis 5:24, Hebrews 11:5).
4. The Old Testament prophet Malachi predicts the return of Elijah.

"Behold, I will send you Elijah the prophet Before the coming of the great and dreadful day of the Lord. And he will turn The hearts of the fathers to the children, And the hearts of the children to their fathers, Lest I come and strike the earth with a curse." (Malachi 4:5-6)

Some scholars suggest that John the Baptist may have been the fulfillment of this Malachi prophecy according to the communication exchange between Jesus and His disciples in Matthew 17:10-13. However, below is a quote from Dr. Henry M. Morris negating this possibility.

"Some assume that this prophecy was fulfilled in John the Baptist, but John the Baptist himself denied it. *"And they asked him, What then? Art thou Elias* (Elijah)? *And he saith, I am not"* (John 1:21). John did indeed come *"in the spirit and power of Elias"* (Luke 1:17), but he was not Elias, and his coming did not fulfill Malachi's prophecy. Jesus Himself confirmed this. *"Elias truly shall first come, and restore all things"* (Matthew 17:11)[62]

Although John did come before the *"great and dreadful day of the Lord,"* the prophetic implication is just prior to this period, rather than over two thousand years beforehand when John existed. Also, John did not *"turn the hearts of the fathers to the children, and the hearts of the children to their fathers."*

5. Moses represents the Law and Elijah the prophets. When the Two Witnesses are on the earth, the Jews are wanting to reinstate the Mosaic Law and its animal sacrificial system. Moses and Elijah would be prime candidates to rebuke this effort. Both know that Jesus Christ is the Messiah. This was evidenced clearly to them at the mount of Transfiguration when the Lord said, *"This is My beloved Son, in whom I am well pleased. Hear Him!"* (Matthew 17:5). Jesus Christ

fulfilled the Law, (Matthew 5:17), and in so doing, He rendered it inoperative. Galatians 3:24 clarifies the purpose of the law. It reads, "Therefore the law was our tutor *to bring us* to Christ, that we might be justified by faith."

6.   There was a dispute between Satan and Michael the archangel over the body of Moses. This could imply that Satan is concerned about Moses returning to the earth again as one of the Two Witnesses, (Jude 1:9).

The Two Witnesses Are The Lord's Rebuttal To The False Covenant

The Two Witnesses arrive on the scene immediately after the false covenant of Daniel 9:27 is confirmed by the Antichrist between Israel and some other party. This book identifies the other probable party as the harlot world religion. The timing of the Two Witnesses arrival and their placement in Jerusalem is strategic. They appear to be the Lord's rebuttal to the dangerous covenant between Israel and the Harlot.

Moses will be able to stand before the Jewish Temple and explain to the Jews that Jesus was the Messiah and that their reinstated animal sacrifices and the Third Temple are not going to atone for their national sins, nor usher in the coming of the Messiah. He will proclaim to them that they must receive Christ as their Messiah, and a remnant of Jews will as per Zechariah 13:9.

Elijah will be able to point out the errors of the Harlot of Roman Catholicism. The Jezebel mentioned in the letter to the Church of Thyatira in Revelation 2:20. The Harlot is killing true believers in Revelation 17:6, just like Jezebel was killing true believers during his time in 1 Kings 18:4.

In the appendix entitled, "The Seven Letters to the Churches," a prophetic connection is made between the Church of Thyatira and Roman Catholicism. As the verses below demonstrate, Thyatira is the church that introduces a demonic feminine character. In fact, it is the only church in the seven letters to do so! The only possible female personage this could represent within the church age is the Catholic version of the Queen of Heaven. These verses below were previously presented in this book, but they deserve repeating and re-paraphrasing.

> "Nevertheless, I have a few things against you, because you allow that woman Jezebel, (*Virgin Mary*), who calls herself a prophetess, (*Marian apparitions often issue prophecies*), to teach and seduce My servants to commit sexual immorality, (*spiritual idolatry*), and eat things sacrificed to idols, (*Transubstantiation in the Eucharist*). And I gave her time to repent of her sexual immorality, and she did not repent, (*Mariology is burgeoning, rather than repenting*). Indeed, I will cast her into a sickbed, and those who commit adultery with her into great tribulation, (*The final three and one-half years of the Trib-Period*), unless they repent of their deeds. I will kill her children with death, and all the churches shall know that I am He who searches the minds and hearts. And I will give to each one of you according to your works." (Rev. 2:20-23; emphasis added)

When Satan read these Thyatira verses about 2000 years ago in correlation with 2 Thessalonians 2:5-12, they probably prompted him to conceive his plan of deception partially through Thyatira, because he realized that this aspect of Christianity would survive the Rapture and be cast into the final days of the Trib-Period. Hence when Pagan Rome morphed into Papal Rome during the Church Age, the devil put his plan of deceit into action. 2 Thessalonians 2 foretold of the time when Satan would be freed from further restraint to deceive mankind.

Thyatira provided the perfect Christian platform to hatch his harlot religious scheme, rather than, in comparison, to the Church of Philadelphia. The letter to the Church of Philadelphia promised that church would be prevented from even entering the Trib-period. Choosing Philadelphia to use Christianity as a platform for deception would have been a poor decision.

"Because you (*Philadelphia*) have kept My command to persevere, I also will keep you from the hour of trial (*Trib-Period*) which shall come upon the whole world, to test those who dwell on the earth." (Rev. 3:10; emphasis added)

Notice the spiritual dichotomy in Satan's scheme. The devil used Bible prophecy to prepare for his campaign of deception. The tip off was that Thyatira would be a good choice, but Philadelphia would be a bad choice. On the flip side, the Lord knowing the future realized that Satan would infiltrate Roman Catholicism and so He reported this in advance within the letter to Thyatira. The letter further states that this Jezebel campaign becomes a church doctrine from the depths of Satan, (Rev. 2:24). The apostle John apparently identified Jezebel of the past, as the representation for the Catholic Virgin Mary of the future because of some of the parallels below.[63]

Jezebel's Traits	End Time Harlot's Traits
A queen - 1 Kings 16:29-31	*A queen* - Revelation 18:7
Encourages idolatry - 1 Kings 21:25-26	*Encourages idolatry* – Rev. 2:20; 17:4
Described as a harlot - 2 Kings 9:22	*Described as a harlot* – Rev. 17:1, 5; 19:2
She uses witchcraft - 2 Kings 9:22	*Uses witchcraft* - Isaiah 47:9, 12; Rev.18:23
Seductress; Outward beauty - 2 Kings 9:30	*Seductress; Outward beauty* - Rev. 17:4
Sheds the saints' blood - 2 Kings 9:7	*Sheds the saints' blood* - Rev. 17:6; 19:2
Massacres God's prophets - 1 Kings 18:4	*Massacres God's prophets* – Rev. 18:24
She is destroyed - 2 Kings 9:33-37	*She is destroyed* - Rev. 17:16; 18:8

A further thematic connection between Jezebel and the Catholic Virgin Mary is goddess worship. Believe it or not, the Queen of Heaven of Roman Catholicism is very much like a goddess to the millions of people who visit her shrines worldwide. They come from all faiths and religions. Here is just one example taken from a news article entitled, "*Twist of globalisation: All faiths come together.*" Below is a quote from this article.

> "*In an unexpected twist of globalisation, Hindus, Buddhists, Muslims and other pilgrims regularly worship at famous Roman Catholic shrines to the Virgin Mary such as Lourdes in France and Fatima in Portugal. They drink the holy water, light votive candles and pray fervently to the Madonna for help with life's hardships. Many venerate her like one of their own goddesses, a view that would be a heresy if a Catholic theologian tried to defend it.*"[64]

Below is a separate quote along these same lines.

> "*Mary was declared to be the "Mother of God" by the Christian church in the 7th century at Ephesus, Turkey. Ephesus was the home of a magnificent temple to the Goddess, Artemis Diana, one of whose sacred titles was "Queen of Heaven". Mary is a more recent and much loved incarnation of the Great Goddess of the ancient Middle-eastern cultures. Mary shares many standard Goddess attributes and symbols.*"[65]

The worship of the goddess Asherah during the time of Elijah was widespread in ancient Israel. In addition to being a personal devotee of Asherah, Jezebel employed 400 prophets that were entirely devoted to this demonic goddess.

> "So go gather all of Israel to meet me on Mount Carmel. Bring along 450 prophets of Baal and

400 prophets of the Asherah who are funded at
Jezebel's expense. (2 Kings 18:19, ISV)

Who was Asherah? Below are a couple quotes that answer this
question.

> *"Asherah was a fertility goddess, the mother of
> Baal. The Asherah existed in both the Southern
> and Northern Kingdoms of Israel. Jezebel of Tyre
> apparently installed Asherah worship in the north
> when she married King Ahab."*[66]

> *" The Book of Jeremiah, written circa 628 BC, possibly
> refers to Asherah when it uses the title "Queen of
> Heaven", stating: "pray thou not for this people…the
> children gather wood, and the fathers kindle the fire,
> and the women knead their dough, to make cakes
> to the Queen of Heaven, and to pour out drink
> offerings to other gods, that they may provoke me to
> anger. (Jeremiah 7:18, 44:17–19, 25)"*[67]

Elijah sounding the alarm about a false Roman Catholic
goddess in the end times would be reminiscent of when he sounded
the alarm in former times of Jezebel's pagan goddess Asherah.

22

The Two Judgments of End Times Babylon

T his chapter is partially taken from the DVD entitled, "*The Identity of Mystery Babylon: Mecca or Rome?*" The DVD was produced from a historic debate between New York Times bestselling author Joel Richardson and myself. Richardson believes that Mecca will be the great harlot city of Revelation 17, and I defended the popular and historic view that the city is Rome.

There are two end times judgments of Babylon in the book of Revelation. Revelation 17:16 makes an end of the Harlot's world religion and Revelation 18:8-10 terminates the global economy. In Richardson's end time scenario, these two judgments are one and the same. If they are not, then in theory his hypothesis about Mecca has significant problems, which will be uncovered at the end of this chapter. However, first, this chapter will explain how these appear to be two distinctly different judgments.

What is the logical chronological order of Revelation 13,17 and 18?

Many people read and interpret the book of Revelation in strict chronological order. They believe that the events of Rev. 13 occur prior to Rev. 17. Others believe that Rev. 17 and 18 describe the same judgment events against Babylon. However, the actual order of events makes most sense when these chapters are rearranged as

Rev. 17, then Rev. 13, then Rev. 18. This sequencing illustrates that Rev. 17 and Rev. 18 are describing two different events with Rev. 13 inserted in-between.

Rev. 17 and Rev. 18 describe judgments upon end times Babylon. However, these two destructions do not appear to be describing the same event. Below is a quote from John Walvoord from his book called, *Every Prophecy of the Bible.*

> *"The Book of Revelation was written in the order in which the truth was revealed to John, but the events described are not necessarily in chronological order... This is especially true of Revelation 17 which probably occurred during the first half of the last seven years... Actually, the destruction of chapter 17 and the destruction of chapter 18 are two separate events by three-and-one-half years."*[68]

Walvoord separates the two events by 3.5 years, meaning the destruction of Rev. 17 happens at the middle of the Tribulation and the destruction of Rev. 18 happens at the end. Below is another related quote about the timing of the differing judgments in Rev. 17 and Rev. 18 from David Guzik.

> *"In my view, it is best to see them as intertwined, yet somewhat distinct. Religious Babylon of Revelation 17 is judged at the mid-point of the seven- year period of tribulation. Commercial Babylon (Rev. 18) is judged at the end of that period."*[69]

Mankind experiences double trouble when it comes to end time Babylon. Two systems occur. First comes the global religion of the great whore in Rev. 17, then comes the beastly commercial system of the Antichrist in Rev. 13. The order of events that are outlined in the Scriptures are summarized below. They demonstrate the Rev. 17, 13,18 sequence.

- *Harlot* forms an alliance with the Antichrist (Rev. 17:3-7)

- *Harlot* rules over a global religious system (Rev. 17:15)

- *Harlot* martyrs' believers in the past and future (Rev. 17:6)

- *10 Kings* hate and desolate the Harlot (Rev. 17:16)

- *10 Kings* transfer their power to the Antichrist (Rev. 17:13,17)

- *Antichrist* then rules over the world (Rev. 13:7-16)

- *Antichrist* sets up a cashless society (Rev. 13:17)

- *Antichrist* martyrs' future believers (Rev. 13:15)

- *Antichrist* kingdom destroyed in 1 hour (Rev. 18:8-10)

- *Antichrist* destroyed by Christ (Rev. 19:11-21)

Rev. 17:15 informs that the Harlot rules worldwide over *"peoples, and multitudes, and nations, and tongues."* At some point this global system becomes problematic for the Antichrist who exerts his power to have the Harlot's false religion eliminated by the infamous Ten Kings. Upon desolating this religious system, they transfer all of its wealth and power over to the Antichrist. This concludes the first judgment of end time Babylon, which deals with the Harlot world religion. The desolation of the Harlot is explained in the verses below.

> "Ten kings receive power as kings one hour with the beast. These have one mind, and shall give their power and strength unto the beast." (Rev. 17:12-13)

> "And the ten horns which you saw on the beast, these will hate the harlot, make her desolate and naked, eat her flesh and burn her with fire. For

God has put it into their hearts to fulfill His purpose, to be of one mind, and to give their kingdom to the beast." (Rev. 17:16-17)

The Ten Kings are of one mind to eliminate the Harlot and to give their kingdom to the Antichrist. From his book, *There's a New World Coming*, Hal Lindsey states the following about this transitional event.

> *"The question that logically comes to mind is, When the Antichrist destroys this Harlot in the middle of the Tribulation, does he destroy some geographical location from which she rules? I personally don't think so, since that would mean destroying his own kingdom, for it is in the Antichrist's kingdom that the Harlot has dominated. For example, if someone today wanted to break the power of the Roman Catholic Church, he wouldn't have to blow up Vatican City or the city of Rome. Assassinations of the Pope and the cardinals and bishops of the church, plus a destruction of some of the major seminaries and church buildings, and a confiscation of church property and wealth would finish the organization. I believe something like this will happen when the Antichrist destroys the false ecclesiastical system that seeks to smother him. He will purge its leaders and confiscate all its wealth. Then he will establish himself as the religious leader of the world and consolidate all worship in himself."[70]*

With the Harlot dethroned in the Middle of the Tribulation, the Antichrist then sets up his global order! Clarence Larkin, (1850-1924 AD), puts it this way below.

> *"The "Ten Kings," finding their power curtailed by the
> "Papal System" will "hate The Whore", and strip her
> gorgeous apparel, confiscate her wealth (eat her flesh)
> and burn her churches and cathedrals with fire. (Rev.
> 17:16). This will occur at the time the worship of the
> Beast is set up in (Rev. 13)."[71]*

At this point the focus shifts from Rev. 17 to Rev. 13. The
Antichrist, who was initially acting in a subservient position to
the Harlot, is now the KING OF THE WORLD. Rev. 17:2 says
the woman was sitting on the beast and in Rev. 17:7 the antichrist
is carrying her to the heights of her global religion. This unholy
alliance stops abruptly with the desolation of the Harlot by the 10
kings. Then we read about the Antichrist's system in Rev. 13.

> "He causes all, both small and great, rich and poor,
> free and slave, to receive a mark on their right
> hand or on their foreheads, and that no one may
> buy or sell except one who has the mark or the
> name of the beast, or the number of his name."
> (Rev. 13:16-17)

With the absence of the Harlot world religion, the Antichrist
assumes worldwide control. He causes all, small, great, rich and
poor to participate in his global order, utilizing a cashless society.
This system is short lived, lasting for only 42 months according to
Rev. 13:5. This period equals the span of the second half of the
7-year tribulation period. And at the end of this three and one-half
years, commercial Babylon is destroyed in "ONE HOUR." Now
we turn our attention to Rev. 18 for the details of this second
judgment upon end times Babylon.

- Antichrist kingdom destroyed in one day (Rev. 18:8)

- Kings of earth lament at their financial losses (Rev. 18:9)

- Babylonian system is destroyed in one hour (Rev. 18:10)

- Merchants of earth can't conduct further commerce (Rev. 18:11)

- Merchants of earth lose all their riches (Rev. 18:12-17)

- Babylon the Great City is utterly destroyed (Rev. 18:19)

- Holy Apostles and prophets are vindicated (Rev. 18:20)

It's important to note from the last bullet point that the city of end time Babylon needs to have been responsible for the martyrdom of at least two or more of the "holy apostles according to the scripture below."

> "Rejoice over her, O heaven, and you holy apostles
> and prophets, for God has avenged you on her!"
> (Rev. 18:20)

History tells us that the Apostle Paul was beheaded in Rome and the Apostle Peter was crucified under the Roman Emperor Nero. In addition, there is historical evidence that the Apostle Andrew was crucified by the order of a Roman governor and the Apostle James, the brother of the Apostle John was killed by a client king of Rome.

This beckons the question, "According to Revelation 18:20, how could this city be Mecca, Saudi Arabia, or other candidate cities like New York City or a rebuilt Babylon in Iraq?

The second destruction of Babylon, which deals with the end of the Antichrist's commercial system is predicted below.

> "Therefore shall her plagues come in one day,
> death, and mourning, and famine; and she shall
> be utterly burned with fire: for strong is the Lord
> God who judgeth her....For in one hour your
> judgment has come.'(Rev. 18:8 and 10, KJV)

"And a mighty angel took up a stone like a great
millstone, and cast it into the sea, saying, Thus
with violence shall that great city Babylon be
thrown down, and shall be found no more at all."
(Rev. 18:21, KJV)

In his book, Revelation Unveiled, Tim LaHaye summarizes
the two sequence of related end times events as follows;

*"The prostitute (religious Babylon) is destroyed
by "beast and the kings of the earth who hate the
prostitute and kill her (Rev.17). This clears the way
for Antichrist to get people to worship him (Rev. 13).
She is destroyed In the middle of the Tribulation;
Babylon, the governmental system will be destroyed
at the end, when commercial Babylon is destroyed
(Rev.18). With Mystery Babylon ..the Mother of
Prostitutes out of the way, all inhabitants of the
earth will worship the beast."* [72]

In summary, the list of distinguished prophecy teachers who
believe these are two separate events and judgments include John
Walvoord, David Guzik, Clarence Larkin, Tim LaHaye, J Vernon
McGee, Hal Lindsey and Mark Hitchcock.

If these Bible teachers are correct in this belief this should
require all eschatological views of end time Babylon to include
two separate, distinct judgments upon the great city of Babylon in
their end time scenarios. This would include even the views of Joel
Richardson and Walid Shoebat, which we are about to look at next.

23

The Mecca – Mystery Babylon Connection and Problems

Now we will look at the Mecca connection to Mystery Babylon according to Joel Richardson. It is important to note that, to the best of my understanding, Joel Richardson believes the following;

1. The Antichrist is a Muslim,
2. Gog of Magog in Ezekiel 38 is the Islamic Antichrist,
3. Gog of Magog comes from Turkey, rather than Russia, which is where most prophecy experts believe Gog hails from.
4. Harlot Religion of Revelation 17 is Islam,
5. Mecca is the "great city" of the Harlot in Revelation 17:18,
6. Ten Kings in Revelation 17:16 are also the Magog invaders of Ezekiel 38:1-5,
7. Ten Kings, as the Magog invaders, destroy the Harlot religion in Rev. 17:16,
8. Magog invasion begins in the first three and one-half years of the Tribulation Period,
9. Antichrist sets his throne up in Jerusalem in the Jewish Temple in the Middle of the Tribulation Period as a result of the Magog invasion,
10. Gog and the Magog invaders get defeated at the end of the seven-year Tribulation Period at the time of Armageddon,

In an article posted on the web entitled, "Mystery Babylon Part 1- The Great Harlot: Revelation 17," Joel Richardson gives us his interpretation of the judgment of the Ten Kings of Revelation 17:16.

> *"The Antichrist and his ten kingdom coalition will bring the Harlot to ruin, They will strip her of her wealth and her royalty and they will literally kill her and burn her with fire."*[73]

From the 2008 book, *God's War on Terror – Islam, Prophecy and the Bible,* by Walid Shoebat and Joel Richardson, Joel and Walid point out that Mecca, as the great city of Mystery Babylon, in addition to Saudi Arabia will be destroyed as part of this judgment.

> *"The idea of Muslims attacking Mecca or Saudi Arabia is far from impossible. The day is drawing near when the emerging Beast Empire led by Turkey and Iran will attack Mecca and destroy the Arabian Harlot...In the Last-Days, a coalition of radical Islamic nations* (alluding to the Magog invaders), *will turn on and destroy Saudi Arabia."*[74]

In fact, an article by Joel Richardson was posted on the World Net Daily website in 2010 with this provocative title, *"Does the Bible Predict Destruction of Saudi Arabia?"* In this article the judgment of Revelation 17:16 was referred to.

Then on page 264 of his book entitled, *Mystery Babylon: Unlocking the Bible's Greatest Prophetic Mystery*, Richardson writes,

> *"Once the Antichrist has consolidated his power over the ten kings, he would turn his attention to Saudi Arabia. In fact, a careful reading of Ezek. 38–39 reveals that this coming Antichrist empire will include Iran, which makes an attack on Saudi Arabia all the more likely. No doubt, this is exactly why the Scriptures declare that "the ten horns . . .*

and the beast, these will hate the harlot and will
make her desolate and naked, and will eat her flesh
and will burn her up with fire" (Rev. 17:16)

And on page 265 of his *Mystery Babylon* book, he continues with,

"Is it possible that the kingdom (Saudi Arabia) could
someday sustain a full-blown nuclear attack? If the oil
fields on the eastern shores of the kingdom were taken
out, it is reasonable to suggest that the entire Western
economy would suffer tremendously, if it survived at
all? Interestingly, such a massive and sudden blow is
certainly in keeping with the description that we find
in the book of Revelation of a city that "in one day . .
. will be burned up with fire" (Rev. 18:8), *never to be*
inhabited again, whose smoke will rise and smolder
"forever and ever" (Rev. 18:21–19:3).

As you can see Joel Richardson has clearly combined the fiery events of Revelation 17:16 and Revelation 18: 8 & 21 into only one destruction event, in which not only the city of Mecca, but the entire nation of Saudi Arabia is apparently destroyed. He suggests the means of the destruction could be a full-blown nuclear attack led by Turkey and Iran and as a result, the city of Mecca will never be inhabited again.

Could Joel and Walid be incorrect in their chronological order of events? What if the correct chronological order of events would require that Revelation 17:16 and Revelation 18:8-10 must be understood to be two entirely separate judgment events, which are separated by the span of at least three and one-half years? Wouldn't this create substantial problems for Joel Richardson and Walid Shoebat in their Islamic end time scenario?

Below is the sequence of events that I believe will happen.

- Harlot forms an unholy alliance with the Antichrist and rules over the nations during the first three and one-half years of the seven-year Tribulation Period in Rev. 17.

- 10 Kings hate and desolate the Harlot and transfer their power to the Antichrist at the mid-point of the seven-year Tribulation period in Rev. 17:13, 16-17.

- Antichrist rules over the world economy once the Harlot is desolated during the remaining second three and one-half years of the Tribulation Period in Rev. 13. This is explained in the verses below.

  "And he (the Antichrist) was given a mouth speaking great things and blasphemies, and he was given authority to continue for forty-two months." (Revelation 13:5). "It was granted to him (the Antichrist) to make war with the saints and to overcome them. And authority was given him over every tribe, tongue, and nation." (Revelation 13:7).

- Antichrist's kingdom is destroyed in one hour on one day forever at the end of the seven-year Tribulation Period in Revelation 18:8-10, 21.

The Mecca as Mystery Babylon Problems

What are the ramifications if the sequence of events just described in my scenario takes place? What are the ramifications if the great city of the Harlot of Mecca in Saudi Arabia will be utterly-destroyed in Revelation 17:16 at the mid-point of the Tribulation Period?

If Mecca gets desolated at the middle of the Tribulation period how will;

1. Muslims worldwide fulfill their required pilgrimage to Mecca during the second half of the Tribulation Period as one of the Five pillars of their Muslim faith?

2. How could they pray toward Mecca 5 times a day?
3. How can these religious Muslims now do their required series of rituals of the hajj performed in and around a city that no longer exists?

Moreover, If God put it in the hearts of the Islamic Antichrist and the ten kings of a coalition of Muslim nations to utterly destroy Mecca at the middle of the Tribulation Period in Revelation 17:16-17, then would this now make it impossible for Mecca to be destroyed again at the end of the Tribulation Period in Rev. 18:8 & 21?

Also, is it likely that after the destruction of Mecca by devout Muslim followers loyal to the Ten Islamic Kings in Revelation 17:16 that the religion of Islam would skyrocket in popularity around the globe and become a worldwide worship movement centered around the worship of an Islamic Antichrist Rev. 13:7?

Another important consideration is that the Ten Kings believe it is necessary to destroy the Harlot in Revelation 17:16 to transfer her power and wealth and to give their kingdom to the Antichrist in Revelation 17:17. This transfer enables the Antichrist to establish his cashless economic system in Revelation 13:15-17. If they are rejoicing over their victory of Mecca and Saudi Arabia at the time of the Harlot's destruction, then why are they weeping in Rev. 18:9 at the judgment of Rev. 18:8, 10?

> "The kings of the earth who committed fornication and lived luxuriously with her will weep and lament for her, when they see the smoke of her burning, standing at a distance for fear of her torment, saying, 'Alas, alas, that great city Babylon, that mighty city! For in one hour your judgment has come.' "And the merchants of the earth will weep and mourn over her, for no one buys their merchandise anymore:" (Rev. 18:8-11)

Although the kings of the earth mentioned in the verses above include more than the Ten Kings, the Ten Kings are likely among those weeping. What goes wrong that causes these kings to weep? In Rev. 17:16 they are rejoicing, but in Rev. 18:8 they are mourning. Rev. 18:9-18 explains that the global economy has been destroyed. That's why the kings and merchants of the earth weep in lament.

This makes logical sense if the Rev. 18:8-10 judgment destroys the Antichrist's global system. As a result of this judgment, no one will be able to buy or sell at that point, even if they did previously take the mark of the Beast in Rev. 13:17. There are no more goods to purchase!

However, Joel Richardson believes that Rev. 18:8-10 is dealing with the destruction of the Harlot's great wealth, which is centered primarily in Saudi Arabia. Below are some quotes from his *Mystery Babylon* book.

> *"The merchants of the earth have grown rich from all the goods that she purchases."* Page 122

> *"Both the" merchants"* (18:3) *and the "shipmaster(s)"* (18:17) *have "become rich through the abundance of her luxury"* (18:3 NKJ) Page 123

> *"The earth's merchants have grown rich from all the goods that she purchases. This is a perfect description of Saudi Arabia."* Page 267

If Joel Richardson is correct that Rev. 18:8,10 represent the same judgment as Rev. 17:16, then the world's economy is decimated when the Ten Kings destroy Saudi Arabia and that leaves the Antichrist with no ability to establish his commercial system. No, it makes more sense that the judgment of Rev. 17:16 happens prior, which provides the Antichrist time and enables him to establish and rule over a global economy. Otherwise, he is left to mop up the mess of the Ten Kings destruction of the harlot and with little to no more time on his hands to do so.

24

Why Jerusalem, New York City and Literal Babylon are not Mystery Babylon

According to Revelation 14:8, 16:19, 17:18, 18:10, 18:16-21, end times Babylon is clearly headquartered in a "Great City." There are five primary candidate cities for the location of the Great City of Mystery Babylon. They are Rome, Mecca, Jerusalem, New York City and historic Babylon.

Some of the arguments for Rome and against Mecca have already been presented in this book. This chapter will identify a few basic problems with Jerusalem, New York City and historic Babylon as the "Great City." Before addressing the potential problems with these three cities, it is important to recognize that there is another convincing argument for Rome as the "Great City."

This additional argument for Rome is found in the understanding of the "Mystery" aspects of end times Babylon.

> "And on her forehead a name *was* written: MYSTERY, BABYLON THE GREAT, THE MOTHER OF HARLOTS AND OF THE ABOMINATIONS OF THE EARTH." (Rev. 17:5)

A biblical mystery in the New Testament is something that was hidden in the Old Testament, but becomes revealed in the New Testament. The revealing can come from different sources. For instance, Christ reveals to the apostle John the mystery of the "Seven Stars and Seven Golden Lampstands."

> "The mystery of the seven stars which you saw in My right hand, and the seven golden lampstands: The seven stars are the angels of the seven churches, and the seven lampstands which you saw are the seven churches." (Rev. 1:20)

In the case of the mystery related with the timing that believers receive their resurrected bodies, the apostle Paul discloses this.

> "Behold, I tell you a mystery: We shall not all sleep, but we shall all be changed in a moment, in the twinkling of an eye, at the last trumpet. For the trumpet will sound, and the dead will be raised incorruptible, and we shall be changed." (1 Corinthians 15:51-52)

Concerning the mystery of the identity of end times Babylon, it is exposed by one of the seven angels who had the seven bowls.

> "But the angel said to me, "Why did you marvel? I will tell you the mystery of the woman, (*BABYLON THE GREAT, THE MOTHER OF HARLOTS*), and of the beast, (*The Antichrist*) that carries her, which has the seven heads and the ten horns."" (Rev. 17:7; emphasis added)

In the Revelation 17:8-18 verses that follow, the angel explains the identities of the Harlot, the Antichrist, the Seven Heads and the Ten Horns. For the purposes of this chapter we will address what the angel divulges about the Harlot.

The reality that this is dealing with a true biblical mystery is proven by the following two important factors:

1. The word mystery is separated from the identity of BABYLON THE GREAT, by a comma in Revelation 17:5, MYSTERY, BABYLON THE GREAT,... Some translations like, the RSV, NIV and the NET go so far as to use a colon to distinctly separate the words of "Mystery" and "Babylon."
2. The angel clearly states in Revelation 17:7, that, "BABYLON THE GREAT, THE MOTHER OF HARLOTS," is indeed a "mystery" that causes the apostle John to marvel with great amazement and needs to be explained.

What the angel reveals about the Harlot is explained in the following three verses.

1. "Here is the mind which has wisdom: The seven heads are seven mountains, (hills in some translations), on which the woman sits." (Rev. 17:9; emphasis added)
2. "Then he said to me, "The waters which you saw, where the harlot sits, are peoples, multitudes, nations, and tongues."" (Rev. 17:15)
3. "And the woman whom you saw is that great city which reigns over the kings of the earth." (Rev. 17:18)

In Revelation 17:18, John discovers that the Harlot is headquartered in a great city. In Revelation 17:9, he learns the geographical location of the great city is upon seven hills. Revelation 17:15 explains that the Harlot has a global reach, that it becomes a religion that is embraced worldwide.

When John received the revelation, Rome was the city that was known as, "The City on Seven Hills." The Romans even minted a coin at the time that featured the "Goddess Roma" sitting on these infamous seven hills.

Most importantly, Revelation 17:18 points out that the *"woman"* John *"saw,"* which represented the past tense, *"is that great city which reigns over the kings of the earth,"* in the present tense.

In other words, at the time John existed, he saw this idolatrous woman with blood stained hands in Revelation 17:1-6. Although she represented a future global religion, he saw this vision, making it a past experience for him. Then, the angel speaks to John in the present and informs him that the great city, "whom you saw," "is" the city that presently reigns over the kings of the earth. From John's perspective that clearly represented the pagan Roman Empire that was headquartered in the city of Rome. John lived during the reign of the Roman Empire.

When John saw the great city of the woman, New York City didn't exist, historic Babylon was essentially in ruins and Jerusalem was under Roman occupation. Some accounts suggest that John authored the book of Revelation near the end of the first century, around A.D. 96. If so, that meant that Jerusalem was desolated and the second Jewish Temple had already been destroyed around A.D. 70.

It is important to note some of the Church Fathers, Reformers and Contemporaries who believe, or have believed, that Rome is the great city of the Harlot identified in Revelation 17:18.

Church Fathers: Lactantius, Tertullian, Irenaeus and Jerome.

Reformers: Martin Luther, John Knox, John Calvin, John Tyndale and John Wycliffe.

Contemporaries: J. Vernon McGee, J. Dwight Pentecost, Clarence Larkin, Grant Jeffrey, Tim LaHaye, Hal Lindsey, Charles Ryrie, Warren Wiersbe, Mike Gendron, Jim Tetlow, Dave Hunt, David Reagan, Ed Hinson, Arno C. Gaebelein, Chuck Smith, Jack Hibbs, Billy Crone and John Phillips.

The Problem with Jerusalem as the Great City of Last Days Babylon

In addition to the fact that Jerusalem was not the city that reigned over the kings of the earth during John's time, there is another major flaw with Jerusalem as a candidate for the great city of end times Babylon.

Revelation 18:21 and elsewhere declares that end times Babylon will ultimately be destroyed. The great city will "be thrown down, and will never be found anymore." This means that mysterious city of last days Babylon has an expiration date. It won't exist during the Millennium.

This would contradict Jeremiah 3:17 and elsewhere, which declares that during the 1000-year Messianic Kingdom period, that the Throne of the Lord will be established in Jerusalem. How could this happen if Jerusalem is destroyed forever and never to be found again?

The Problem with New York City as the Great City of Last Days Babylon

New York City, (NYC), has several problems.

1. It doesn't sit on "Seven Hills," (Rev. 17:9).
2. Two or more of the "Holy Apostles" were never killed there, (Rev. 18:20).
3. It didn't exist as a city that ruled over the kings of the earth during John's time, (Rev. 17:18).

Revelation 17:9 mandates that the great city be geographically located upon seven hills. New York City does not meet this requirement. To get around this glaring problem, some who advocate for NYC have suggested that the seven hills are actually seven continents. The Greek word used for hills in Rev. 17:9 is "Oros," which means hills or mountains.

Top Bible scholars from the NLT, NIV, CEV, AMP, GNT, CJB, NJB and NAB Bible translations have closely looked at the biblical text in Revelation 17:9 and have determined that the Greek word "Oros" should be interpreted as "hills." The Strong's Concordance #3735 defines that "Oros" is best rendered as hills or mountains, but says nothing about continents.

Moreover, New York City was founded in A.D. 1624, which means two things;

1. It did not rule over the kings of the earth at the time it was revealed to the apostle John that the great city he "saw" in Rev. 17:18, "is that great city which reigns over the kings of the earth."
2. There were no holy apostles alive when NYC was founded. The holy apostles that are vindicated when end times Babylon is destroyed in Revelation 18:20, were all martyred about 16-centuries prior to the founding of NYC.

The point that Revelation 18:20 requires the death of two or more of the holy apostles was already mentions earlier within this book.

> "Rejoice over her, O heaven, and you holy apostles, (Plural, alluding to two or more), and prophets, for God has avenged you on her!" (Rev. 18:20, NKJV; emphasis added)

> "Rejoice over her, you heavens! Rejoice, you people of God! Rejoice, apostles and prophets! For God has judged her with the judgment she imposed on you." (Rev. 18:20, NIV)

The Problem with Historic Babylon as the Great City of Last Days Babylon

Some believe that historic Babylon will be rebuilt in the last days to the stature of the great city of Rev. 17:18. They often site the city of Dubai as an example of a city that could be built in a relatively short order of time. Dubai emerged as a city relatively recently and in approximately the span of 20-years.

However, the rebuilding of historic Babylon to the stature of a great city is unlikely. Iraq, where literal Babylon existed, has mostly become a war-torn area in modernity. Additionally, there are ongoing struggles for control over Iraq between the Shiite and Sunni factions within Islam.

Another problem for a rebuilt literal Babylon scenario, is that the identity of last days Babylon in Rev. 17:5 is dealing with a mystery, rather than a reality. The verse does not read, REALITY, BABYLON THE GREAT, THE MOTHER OF HARLOTS AND OF THE ABOMINATIONS OF THE EARTH.

If end times Babylon was dealing with the literal historic Babylon, the usage of the word mystery would not have made sense to John. He was familiar with the literal Babylon of the Old Testament, but the fact that end times Babylon was a mystery, means that the identity was concealed in the Old Testament, rather than revealed.

Lastly, historic Babylon was not responsible for the killing of two or more of the holy apostles, which is required as per Rev. 18:20. Babylon was conquered by King Cyrus of Persia around 539 B.C., which was over 5-centuries prior to the deaths of the apostles of Jesus Christ. During the reign of the Babylonian Empire between 626 – 539 B.C. the holy apostles of Christ didn't even exist.

Appendices

1

The Revised Apocalyptic Timeline

The appendix provides a timeline for the unfulfilled biblical predictions of the last days. It is formatted to correspond closely with the books in this end time's trilogy, which are, *Revelation Road, Apocalypse Road* and *Tribulation Road*.[75] These three books are identified and bracketed in their appropriate time slots directly beneath the timeline.

NOW, NEXT and LAST Prophecies

There are three categories of coming biblical prophecies. They are the;

1. *NOW Prophecies*, which are covered in *Revelation Road*.
2. *NEXT Prophecies*, which are covered in *Apocalypse Road*.
3. *LAST Prophecies*, which will be covered in *Tribulation Road*.

The *NOW Prophecies* are the unfulfilled ancient biblical predictions that appear to be imminent, which means they could happen NOW! These ancient foretellings have either minor or no remaining preconditions inhibiting them from happening at the present time. These predictions are identified and explained in detail within my book entitled, "*The Now Prophecies*."

The *NEXT Prophecies* are those that follow the fulfillment of the NOW Prophecies. In essence, the NOW's provide the necessary nexus of events that pave the path for the execution of the NEXT Prophecies. Although the NEXT Prophecies are rapidly racing toward fulfillment, they require the completion of the NOW's in order for their stage to become appropriately set.

The *LAST Prophecies* still have significant preconditions preventing them from finding fulfillment. They will find fulfillment relatively soon, but the LAST's have to wait in line behind the NOW's and NEXT's for their turn on the prophetic timeline.

The image below includes the numbers between #1 through #8 that identify the probable timing of the unfulfilled prophecies listed beneath the timeline. These numbers are sequenced in the three primary periods of the last days, which are;

1. *The Church age*, which ends with the Rapture.
2. *The Post-Rapture / Pre-Tribulation Gap Period*, which begins immediately after the Rapture and concludes when the seven-year Tribulation period, (Trib-period), starts.
3. *The Seven-Year Tribulation Period*, which concludes with the Second Coming of Christ.

CAVEAT: In no way, does this timeline appendix attempt to set a date, time or any preconditions for the fulfillment of the Rapture prophecy. I believe that the Rapture is an imminent event that could happen at any time between now and the start of the seven-year Trib-period. It is a sign-less event, which means that the prophecy has no preconditions!

Apocalypse Road Timeline

The prophecies below are listed in the chronological order that the I believe they could happen. However, these events might find fulfillment differently than they are sequenced. Moreover, these predictions only represent some of, rather than all of, the prophecies of the end times. Each prediction begins with its time slot between numbers #1 through #8.

#1-Time Slot: The Church Age

The **#1-time slot** concludes with the Rapture. Thus, all of these prophecies in the #1-time slot automatically shift to the **#2**-time slot of the Post-Rapture / Pre-Tribulation Gap Period, if they have not found fulfillment prior to the Rapture.

#1- Disaster in Iran – (Jeremiah 49:34-39),

#1- Destruction of Damascus – (Isaiah 17, Jer. 49:23-27),

#1- Final Arab-Israeli War- (Psalm 83),

#1- Toppling of Jordan – (Jer. 49:1-6, Zephaniah 2:8-10, Ezekiel 25:14),

#1- Terrorization of Egypt – (Isaiah 19:1-18),

#1- Expansion of Israel – (Obadiah 1:19-20, Jer. 49:2, Zephaniah 2:9, Isaiah 19:18),

#1- Vanishing of the Christians – (1 Corinthians 15:51-52, 1 Thessalonians 4:15-18).

#2-Time Slot: The Post-Rapture / Pre-Tribulation Gap Period

Some of the **#2-time slot** begin in the #2 slot, but conclude in a subsequent time slot.

#2- Ezekiel 38; the Gog of Magog war, (Ezekiel 39-39),

#2- Supernatural signs and lying wonders from Satan, (2 Thess. 2:9),

#2- The 144,000 Jewish Witnesses emerge, (Rev. 7:1-8),

#2- First Seal: The White Horseman; the Antichrist, (Rev. 6:1-2),

#2- Second Seal: The Red Horseman; wars, (Rev. 6:3-4),

#2- Third Seal: The Black Horseman; famines, (Rev. 6:5-6),

#2- Fourth Seal: The Pale Horsemen; Death and Hades, (Rev. 6:7-8),

#2- Fifth Seal: The martyrdom of Christians, (Rev. 6:9-11),

#2- The Harlot World Religion emerges, (Rev. 17).

#2- The Overflowing Scourge Begins, (Isaiah 28:15)

#3-6 Time Slots: The Seven-Year Tribulation Period

The Tribulation Period begins when the false covenant of Daniel 9:27 gets confirmed. This period is also referred to in the Bible as Daniel's Seventieth Week.

#3- The False Covenant Gets Confirmed by the Antichrist, (Daniel 9:27)

#3- The opening of the 6th and 7th Seal judgments, (Rev. 6:12-17 and Rev. 8:1),

#3- The sounding of the seven Trumpet judgments, (Rev. 8-9),

#3- The ministry of the 2 Witnesses, (Rev. 11:1-12),

#3- The building of the 3rd Jewish Temple, (Rev. 11:1-2),

#4- War in heaven and casting out of Satan and the fallen angels from heaven, (Rev. 12:7-9),

#4- The desolation of the Harlot World Religion, (Rev. 17:16),

#4- The killing and resurrection of the 2 Witnesses, (Rev. 11:1-12),

#4- The Abomination of Desolation, (Matthew 24:15),

#4- The campaign of Jewish genocide by the Antichrist begins, (Zechariah 13:8),

#4- The Mark of the Beast campaign by the False Prophet and the Antichrist, (Rev. 13:14-18),

#5- The pouring out of God's wrath in the seven Bowl judgments, (Rev. 16),

#5- The Armageddon campaign, (Joel 3:2, Rev. 16:6),

#5- The complete destruction of commercial Babylon, (Rev 18:8-10,21),

#5- The Remnant of Israel receives Christ as their Messiah, (Hosea 5:15, Matt. 23:39),

#6- The Second Coming of Christ, (Isaiah 63:1-6 and Matt. 24:30),

#6- The destruction of the Antichrist and his armies, (Daniel 11:45, 2 Thess. 2:8).

#7-8 Time Slots: The 75-day interval period and the Millennium

#7- Christ's victory ascent to the Mount of Olives, (Zechariah 14:4),

#7- The Sheep and Goat gentile judgments, (Matt. 25:31-46),

#8- The 1000-year millennial reign of Christ, (Rev. 20:4).

2
The Seven Letters to the Churches

The seven letters to the seven churches in Revelation 2 and 3 have multiple applications. First, they were instructional for the seven actual churches existing at the time. Second, similarities of these types of churches could be found throughout the church age. Third, these letters had a prophetic application. They were intended to chronologically order the seven stages of church development throughout its earthly existence.

Fortunately, we have the advantage of looking back upon church history, which enables us to determine each church period. Below is an outline of the chronological development of the Christian church in accordance with the blueprints of the seven letters in Revelation. This outline reveals that we are living in the final days of church development, the "days of Laodicea."

Ephesus (Revelation 2:1-7; AD 40-150) The first stage of Christianity was primarily an apostolic period. Christians operated in compliance with Matthew 28:18-20. It was a time of reconciliation wherein the disciples successfully preached the good news gospel of Jesus Christ outwardly from Jerusalem into the surrounding Gentile populations of the world. This was Christianity in its infancy, and as a religion it was rapidly spreading throughout the broader Middle East region and into the greater Roman Empire.

Smyrna (Revelation 2:8-11; AD 100-312) This segment of church history was characterized by a period of persecution. Rome was conducting wide-scale Christian executions in an attempt to prevent the growth and spread of the religion. Martyrdom was the unfortunate predicament forced upon the church by the Roman

Empire (Pagan Rome) during the Smyrna era. However, to Rome's chagrin, the persecutions actually bolstered the growth of Christianity. Christians dying for their faith caught the attention of multitudes that in turn fixated their focus upon Christ as their Savior.

Pergamos (Revelation 2:12-17; AD 300-600) The period of Pergamos, meaning "mixed marriage" in Greek, is associated with the paganization of the church. As the Roman Empire began its decline, it embraced Christianity as its state religion. This served two primary purposes. First, it began to fill deepening political rifts developing in the deteriorating Roman government; and secondly, it facilitated the survival of faltering pagan religious practices by cleverly integrating and incubating them into Christianity. Also, the martyrdom period of Smyrna that experienced Christianity flourishing became problematic for Rome. Each martyr's death brought new and renewed strength among fellow Christians. Thus, Rome adopted the attitude, "If you can't beat them [kill all the Christians], join them."

As time passed this Roman attitude eventually led many Christians to reciprocate and romanticize Romanism, and to believe that "*When in Rome, do as the Romans do.*" During the Pergamos period, Christianity essentially was asked to compromise itself—and in so doing, created an end to the persecutions occurring during the Smyrna stage. By marrying up with Roman paganism, an adulterated version of Christianity insured its survival. Shortly thereafter, ancient Roman religious practices began to permeate the church. Christian traditions, such as Christmas trees and Yule logs, can likely be traced to this Pergamos period of church history.

Thyatira (Revelation 2:18-29; AD 600-Tribulation) This church is commonly thought to represent the Roman Catholic Church, (Papal Rome), which evolved out of the Pergamos period. Thyatira tends to be a works-based, rather than a faith-based church. In so doing it emphasizes the religious rather than relational importance between God and humanity. Revelation 2:22 declares that an apostate element within Thyatira will exist in the end times and be cast into the "sickbed" of the great tribulation period.

"Nevertheless I have a few things against you, (The Roman Catholic Church), because you allow that woman, (The Queen of Heaven), Jezebel, who calls herself a prophetess, to teach and seduce My servants to commit sexual immorality and eat things sacrificed to idols. And I gave her time to repent of her sexual immorality, and she did not repent. Indeed I will cast her into a sickbed, and those who commit adultery with her into great tribulation, unless they repent of their deeds. I will kill her children with death, and all the churches shall know that I am He who searches the minds and hearts. And I will give to each one of you according to your works." (Revelation 2:20-23, emphasis added).

The comparisons between Jezebel and the Blessed Mother of Roman Catholicism are made in the chapter called, "The Two Witnesses."

Sardis (Revelation 3:1-6; AD 1500-Tribulation) This period is best described as the Protestant Reformation; however, it lacked true transformation. Salvation through faith rather than works was reintroduced within Christianity; however, the Reformation continued to be more about religion than about a personal relationship with God.

Philadelphia (Revelation 3:7-13; AD 1800-Rapture) Philadelphia means "*brotherly love.*" Powerful, worldwide missionary movements beginning in the mid-1600s characterize the period of Philadelphia. In accordance with Matthew 28:18-20, this church answered the call to the "Ministry of Reconciliation." The Philadelphian period concludes with the rapture as per Revelation 3:10, which says that this church will be kept from "*the hour of trial which shall come upon the whole world,*" alluding to the Trib-period.

Laodicea (Revelation 3:14-22; AD 1900-Tribulation) Laodicea means "*people's rights.*" Inherent in its name is the inference that this is a church predominately ruled by the people rather than the Lord. This church began in the twentieth century and will continue into the seven-year tribulation period. Laodicea believes that it is a prosperous church having need of nothing; conversely, Christ considers it *"wretched, miserable, poor, blind, and naked,"* (Rev. 3:17). IN Rev. 3:18, Christ encourages this church to abandon its apostate practices and purchase gold from Him that is refined through the fire. By the reference to gold refined through fire, Christ implies that Laodicea is an impure and undisciplined church in need of repentance.

Laodicea treats Christ more like an ordinary stranger, rather than an extraordinary Savior. They position Him mostly outside the church, which causes Him to say,

> "Behold, I stand at the door and knock. If anyone
> hears My voice and opens the door, I will come
> in to him and dine with him, and he with Me."
> (Rev. 3:20)

Most Bible prophecy teachers believe that these are the days of Laodicea.

3
IRAN is in Ezekiel 38, but why NOT their PROXIES?

Why are Syria, Hezbollah, Hamas and the Houthis MISSING IN ACTION?

Ezekiel 38:5 lists Persia, renamed Iran in 1935, as a member of the Magog coalition that invades Israel in the latter days.

> Persia, Ethiopia, and Libya are with them, (*Magog Coalition*), all of them *with* shield and helmet. (Ezekiel 38:5)

The fifty-two verses in Ezekiel 38-39 provide some of the most literally descriptive predictions within the entire Bible. It identifies the invaders, their motives, their defeats, the Lord's divine intervention and purposes and the sequence of aftermath events. The focus of this article is the identification of WHO IS and WHO IS NOT, part of Ezekiel 38-39.

WHO IS PART OF THE EZEKIEL 38 PROPHECY

Ezekiel 38 and 39 involves at least fourteen participants in the prophecy. They are;

1. *The Victor:* God.
2. *The (intended) Victim:* Israel.
3. *The Invaders:* Magog, Meshech, Tubal, Persia, Ethiopia, Libya, Gomer, and Togarmah. (Refer to the Ezekiel 38 map image on page 110 to find out the consensus of the modern-day equivalents of the Magog coalition. Image designed by Lani Harmony Salhus).
4. *The Protestors:* Sheba, Dedan, the merchants of Tarshish and their Young Lions.

The prophecy informs that, in the latter years the invaders will attack Israel to capture plunder and booty. They covet Israel's economic prosperity and conspire militarily to confiscate this livelihood as part of their spoils of war. As the victor, the Lord, not the IDF or America, prevents this from occurring by utilizing supernatural means to defeat these invaders. These miraculous events are described in Ezekiel 38:18-39:6.

Meanwhile, as the epic event unfolds, the protestors complain about the evil intentions of the invaders. Their protests are lodged in the questions in Ezekiel 38:13 quoted below.

> "Sheba, Dedan, the merchants of Tarshish, and all their young lions will say to you, 'Have you come to take plunder? Have you gathered your army to take booty, to carry away silver and gold, to take away livestock and goods, to take great plunder?'" (Ezekiel 38:13)

Ultimately, after the invaders are conquered, Israel graduates from being the intended victim and instead becomes the resultant benefactor. The modern-day equivalents of these protestors today are commonly understood and taught to be;

1.   *Sheba*: Yemen, where the Iranian proxies, the Houthis, exist today.
2.   *Dedan*: Saudi Arabia and perhaps parts of the Gulf Cooperative Council (GCC) Arab Gulf States.
3.   *Tarshish*: Either the UK or Spain.
4.   *Young Lions*: Either the colonies that came from the UK, namely North America, or the offshoots of Spain, mainly the Latin American countries. (In my book entitled, *The Now Prophecies*, I explain why the "*Tarshish*" is likely the UK and their "*Young Lions*" seems to be America.

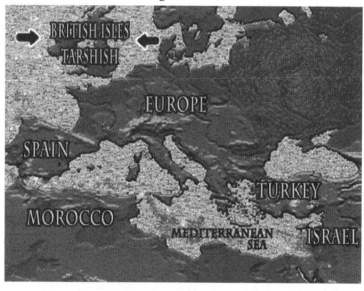

WHO IS NOT PART OF THE EZEKIEL 38 PROPHECY

Having identified WHO IS part of the action in Ezekiel 38-39, now let's observe who appears to be MISSING IN ACTION (MIA). The emphasis is put upon Iran and its present proxies, who are, Hezbollah, Syria, Hamas and the Houthis. Iran also has a burgeoning presence within Iraq.

THE HOUTHIS

Iran-aligned Houthis in Yemen fire missiles at Saudi capital – *Reuters 5/8/18*

> "*Yemen's Houthis fired a salvo of ballistic missiles at Saudi Arabia's capital on Wednesday - an attack Saudi authorities said they intercepted in the skies over Riyadh. The assault took place a day after Saudi Arabia's top Western ally the United States pulled out of a deal with Iran over its disputed nuclear program and could signal an uptick in tensions between Riyadh and regional rival Tehran.*" [76]

The Houthis are busy helping Iran spread its hegemony throughout the Middle East. Some suspect the Houthis, who were given missiles by Iran, are testing the proficiency of these missiles, by using Saudi Arabia as a punching bag. The purpose in part, is to confirm that Hezbollah's 150,000 Iranian provided missiles will be effective against a war with Israel.

At the very least, it is observable that the Houthis in Yemen are currently enemies of the Saudis. Yet, in Ezekiel 38:13, we see that Yemen, as Sheba, and Saudi Arabia, as Dedan, are aligned together protesting Iran's participation in the Magog invasion of Israel. The glaring question is: "*Why is Yemen not included among the Magog invaders?*" The probable answer is that something adverse happens to the Houthis before Ezekiel 38, that eliminates them as an affective proxy of Iran.

HEZBOLLAH

Iran hails 'victory against Israel' by its proxy Hezbollah in Lebanon elections – *Times of Israel 5/8/18*

> *"A senior Iranian official on Tuesday hailed the "victory" of the Hezbollah terrorist group in Lebanese elections as a success in the "fight against Israel" and the United States."[77]*

Hezbollah is a major threat to Israel. Estimates are that they have about 150,000 advanced missiles pointed at a bank of strategic Israeli targets. Some analysts suspect that when Iran gives its Hezbollah proxy the green light to war against Israel, that with the number of launchers they have, could launch 1000 missiles per day into the Jewish state.

Yet, we see no resemblance of Hezbollah mentioned among the Ezekiel invaders. Hezbollah hails from Lebanon, and if they were part of the Ezekiel prophecy, they would likely be identified by the biblical names for Lebanon, which are Lebanon, Tyre, Sidon, or Gebal. None of these names are listed in Ezekiel 38, however, Tyre and Gebal are listed in the Psalm 83 prophecy.

The question is: *"Why isn't Lebanon, Tyre, Sidon or Gebal listed alongside Persia in Ezekiel 38:1-6?"* In his forty-eight chapters Ezekiel refers to these places at least twenty-times, but not even an honorable mention in Ezekiel 38-39. Additionally, perplexing, is the fact that Ezekiel 38:15 and 39:2 specify that the Magog invaders attack from the North of Israel, which is the actual geographic location of Hezbollah in Lebanon.

Perhaps like the Houthis, Hezbollah has something crippling happen to this terrorist group that eliminates it from the Magog invasion.

SYRIA

Israel strikes Iranian targets in Syria after rocket fire – *Reuters 5/9/18*

> *"It was the heaviest Israeli barrage in Syria since the 2011 start of the civil war in which Iranians, allied*

> *Shi'ite Muslim militias and Russian troops have*
> *deployed in support of President Bashar al-Assad.*
> *The confrontation came two days after the United*
> *States announced its withdrawal, with Israel's*
> *urging, from a nuclear accord with Iran.*"[78]

Iran has been instrumental in supporting President Bashar al-Assad of Syria throughout the Syrian revolution. Yet, there is no mention of Syria, Assyria, Damascus, Hamath or Arpad among the Magog Invaders. These are the biblical names for modern-day Syria. Ezekiel alludes to these names at least twelve times in his forty-eight chapters, but not once in Ezekiel 38.

However, Assyria shows up in the Psalm 83 prophecy. Damascus is destroyed in the prophecies within Isaiah 17, and Damascus, Hamath and Arpad are the subjects of Jeremiah 49:23-27. "*Why isn't Syria listed alongside Iran in Ezekiel 38?*" Is it because Damascus gets destroyed in Isaiah 17 beforehand?

HAMAS

HAMAS AND IRAN CLOSEST THEY'VE BEEN SINCE SYRIAN WAR, SENIOR OFFICIAL SAYS – *Jerusalem Post* *3/28/18*[79]

As this Jerusalem Post headline points out, Hamas is another Iranian proxy terrorist group. Hamas is located in the ancient biblical lands of Philistia or Gaza among other names. Although Philistia is identified in Psalm 83:7, it is nowhere to be found in Ezekiel 38-39. "*Why not?*" Is it because Psalm 83 finds fulfillment prior to Ezekiel 38? Is that also why Hezbollah and Assyria are not part of Ezekiel 38? All three of these Iranian proxies today, were aligned together in the 3000-year old prophecy of Psalm 83.

> They have said, "Come, and let us cut them
> off from *being* a nation, That the name of
> Israel may be remembered no more." For they

have consulted together with one consent; They form a confederacy against You: The tents of Edom and the Ishmaelites; Moab and the Hagrites; **Gebal**, Ammon, and Amalek; **Philistia** with the inhabitants of **Tyre**; **Assyria** also has joined with them; They have helped the children of Lot. (Psalm 83:4-8)

DOES PSALM 83 PRECEDE EZEKIEL 38? IS THAT WHY THESE IRANIAN PROXIES ARE MISSING IN ACTION IN THE EZEKIEL 38-39 PROPHECIES? For more information about this possibility, read my article entitled, "Psalm 83 or Ezekiel 38, Which is the Next Middle East News Headline."[80] Below is a map designed by Lani Harmony Salhus of the Inner Circle of the Psalm 83 confederacy. These are Israel's notorious enemies. Compare this to the Outer Ring map of the Ezekiel 38 coalition, who have never been Israel's historical enemies. (See map of the "Inner Circle" on page 110)

REVEALING IRAN'S DOUBLE JEOPARDY

Many of you may not recognize that Iran is the subject of two latter days prophecies. Jeremiah 49:34-39, which identifies Iran as Elam and Ezekiel 38:5, which mentions Iran as Persia. Ancient maps of modern-day Iran reveal these two separate territories. The Jeremiah Elam prophecy, in my estimation, appears to be dealing with Iran's present nuclear scenario, and I believe it could happen NOW!

If you want to learn more about the vastly overlooked Jeremiah prophecy of Elam, you can read my book or watch my DVD entitled. Nuclear Showdown in Iran, Revealing the Ancient Prophecy of Elam.

4

The Sinner's Salvation Prayer

"In an acceptable time I have heard you, And in the day of salvation I have helped you." Behold, now *is* the accepted time; behold, now *is* the day of salvation. (2 Corinthians 6:2)

"And you shall love the Lord your God with all your heart, with all your soul, with all your mind, and with all your strength. This *is* the first commandment.""* (Mark 12:30)

The most important decision one can make in their entire lifetime is to receive Christ as their personal Lord and Savior. It is the sinner's passport to paradise! It's an all-inclusive package that provides a forgiven and changed life on earth now and a guaranteed future admission into heaven afterward.

Without God's forgiveness, the sinner cannot enter into heaven because earthly sin is not allowed to exist there. Otherwise, it would not be rightfully called "heaven." Jesus was sent into the world to provide a remedy for man's sin problem. The Bible teaches that we are all sinners and that the wages, (what we deserve), of sin is death, (spiritual separation from God forever). But God so loved us that He wanted to make a way so anyone could be forgiven and thus be allowed to enter heaven. God doesn't want anyone to perish, and has been patient with us so that we can turn from sin and find forgiveness, (by faith), in His son, Jesus.

"For God so loved the world that He gave His only begotten Son, [*Jesus Christ*] that whoever believes

in Him should not perish but have everlasting
life." (John 3:16, NKJV).

"And this is eternal life, that they may know You, the
only true God, and Jesus Christ [*Begotten Son of
God*] whom You have sent." (John 17:1-3, NKJV).

These passages point out that people are perishing to the great
displeasure of God, who loves them immeasurably. He wishes that
none would perish, but that everyone would inhabit eternity with
Him and His only begotten Son, Jesus Christ. Quintessential to
eternal life is the knowledge of these two concepts.

Sin Separates Us from the Love of God

The apostle John reminds us in 1 John 4:8, 16 that God is
love, but man lives in a condition of sin, which separates him from
God's love. Romans 8:5-8 explains how sin manifests into carnal
behavior that creates enmity between God and man.

"So then, those who are in the flesh cannot please
God." (Romans 8:8, NKJV).

The book of Romans instructs that sin entered into the world
through Adam, and spread throughout all mankind thereafter.
Additionally, Romans informs that sin is the root cause of death,
but through Jesus Christ eternal life can be obtained.

"Therefore, just as through one man [*Adam*] sin
entered the world, and death through sin, and
thus death spread to all men, because all [*men*]
sinned." (Romans 5:12; emphasis added).

"All we like sheep have gone astray; We [*mankind*]
have turned, every one, to his own way; And the
LORD has laid on Him [*Jesus Christ*] the iniquity
of us all." (Isaiah 53:6; emphasis added).

"For the wages of sin *is* death, but the gift of God *is* eternal life in Christ Jesus our Lord." (Romans 6:23, NKJV).

If this makes sense to you, and you:

1.   Have humbled yourself to recognize that you are a sinner, living under the curse of sin, which has separated you from your Creator.
2.   Believe that Jesus Christ took your punishment for sin so that you could be pardoned, as the only way to be saved.
3.   Want to repent and start letting God make changes in your life to be in a right relationship with God,
4.   And, want to do it right now,

Then you have come to the right place spiritually. It is the place where millions before you, and many of your contemporaries alongside you, have arrived.

Fortunately, you have only one final step to take to complete your eternal journey. This is because salvation is a gift of God. Christ paid the full price for all sin, past, present, and future, when He sacrificed His life in Jerusalem about 2000 years ago. Your pardon for sin is available to you through faith in the finished work of Jesus Christ, which was completed upon His bloodstained cross. His blood was shed on our behalves. He paid sins wages of death on our account.

You must now take the final leap of faith to obtain your eternal salvation. It is your faith in Christ that is important to God.

"But without faith *it is* impossible to please [*God*] *Him*, for he who comes to God must believe that He is, and *that* He is a rewarder of those who diligently seek Him." (Hebrews 11:6, NKJV; emphasis added).

"In this you [*believer*] greatly rejoice, though now
for a little while, if need be, you have been grieved
by various trials, that *the genuineness of your faith,
being much more precious than gold that perishes,*
though it is tested by fire, may be found to praise,
honor, and glory at the revelation of Jesus Christ,
whom having not seen you love. Though now
you do not see *Him,* yet believing, you rejoice
with joy inexpressible and full of glory, receiving
the end of your faith—the salvation of *your* souls."
(1 Peter 1:6-9, NKJV).

Before the necessary step to salvation gets introduced it is
important to realize and appreciate that salvation is a gift provided
to us through God's grace. We didn't earn our salvation, but we must
receive it. If you are one who has worked hard to earn everything
you have achieved in life then you are to be commended. However,
apart from living a sinless life, which is humanly impossible, there
is nothing you as a sinner could have done to meet the righteous
requirement to cohabitate in eternity with God. In the final analysis,
when we see our Heavenly Father in His full glory, we will all be
overwhelmingly grateful that Christ's sacrificial death bridged the
chasm between our unrighteousness, and God's uncompromised
holiness.

"But God, who is rich in mercy, because of His
great love with which He loved us, even when
we were dead in [*sin*] trespasses, made us alive
together with Christ (*by grace you have been saved*),
and raised *us* up together, and made *us* sit together
in the heavenly *places* in Christ Jesus, that in the
ages to come He might show the exceeding riches
of His grace in *His* kindness toward us in Christ
Jesus. *For by grace you have been saved* through
faith, and that not of yourselves; *it is the gift of
God,* not of works, lest anyone should boast."
(Ephesians 2:4-9; emphasis added).

The Good News Gospel Truth

The term gospel is derived from the Old English *"god-spell,"* which has the common meaning *"good news,"* or *"glad tidings."* In a nutshell, the gospel is the good news message of Jesus Christ. Jesus came because God so loved the world that He sent His Son to pay the penalty for our sins. That's part of the good news, but equally important is the "Resurrection."

This is the entire good news gospel;

> "For I delivered to you first of all that which I also received: that Christ died for our sins according to the Scriptures, and that He was buried, and that He rose again the third day according to the Scriptures." (1 Corinthians 15:3-4; NKJV).

Christ resurrected which means He's alive and able to perform all of His abundant promises to believers. The Bible tells us that He is presently in heaven seated at the right-hand side of God the Father waiting until His enemies become His footstool. Furthermore, from that position Christ also intercedes on the behalf of Christians. This intercession is an added spiritual benefit to you for becoming a believer.

> "But this Man, [*Jesus Christ became a Man, to die a Man's death*] after He had offered one sacrifice for sins forever, sat down at the right hand of God, from that time waiting till His enemies are made His footstool. For by one offering He has perfected forever those who are being sanctified." (Hebrews 10:12-14; emphasis added).

> "Who *is* he who condemns? *It is* Christ who died, and furthermore is also risen, who is even at the right hand of God, who also makes intercession for us." (Romans 8:34)

The resurrection of Christ overwhelmingly serves as His certificate of authenticity to all His teachings. He traveled through the door of death, and resurrected to validate His promises and professions. This can't be said of the claims of Buddha (Buddhism), Mohammed (Islam), Krishna (Hinduism), or any of the other host of deceased, human, non-resurrected, false teachers. All the erroneous teachings they deposited on the living side of death's door were invalidated when they died and lacked the power to conquer death itself, as Jesus has done.

One of Christ's most important claims is;

> "Jesus said to him, "I am the way, the truth, and the life. No one comes to the [*heavenly*] Father except through Me."" (John 14:6; emphasis added).

This is a critical claim considering eternal life can only be obtained by knowing the heavenly Father, and Christ, whom He [the Father] sent, according to John 17, listed earlier in this chapter. Most importantly, the resurrection proves that death has an Achilles heel. It means that its grip can be loosed from us, but only by Christ who holds the power over death.

> "*O Death, where is your sting? O Hades, where is your victory?*" The sting of death *is* sin, and the strength of sin *is* the law. But thanks *be* to God, who gives us the victory [*over Death and Hades*] through our Lord Jesus Christ." (1 Corinthian 15:55-57; emphasis added).

How to be Saved – You Must Be Born Again

> "Jesus answered and said to [*Nicodemus*] him, "Most assuredly, I say to you, unless one is born again, he cannot see the kingdom of God.""(John 3:3; emphasis added).

Jesus told Nicodemus, a religious leader of his day, that entrance into the kingdom of god required being born again. This is a physical impossibility, but a spiritual necessity, and why faith plays a critical role in your salvation. You can't physically witness your new birth; it is a spiritual accomplishment beyond your control that happens upon receiving Christ as your Lord and Savior. God takes full responsibility for your metamorphosis into a new creation at that point.

> "Therefore, if anyone *is* in Christ, *he is* a new creation; old things have passed away; behold, all things have become new." (2 Corinthians 5:17, NKJV).

You must trust God to perform on His promise to escort you through the doors of death into eternity, and to process you into the likeness of Christ. This is the ultimate meaning of being born again, and alongside Christ, is a responsibility undertaken by the third member of the Trinity, the Holy Spirit. Christ holds the power over Death and Hades, but the Holy Spirit is your "*Helper*" that participates in your spiritual processing.

> "I *am* He [*Jesus Christ*] who lives, and was dead, and behold, I am alive forevermore. [*Resurrected*] Amen. And I have the keys of Hades and of Death." (Revelation 1:18; emphasis added).

> "If you love [*Christ*] Me, keep My commandments. And I will pray the Father, and He will give you another Helper [*Holy Spirit*], that He may abide with you forever— the Spirit of truth, whom the world cannot receive, because it neither sees Him nor knows Him; but you know Him, for He dwells with you and will be in you." (John 14:15-17; emphasis added).

> "These things I have spoken to you while being present with you. But the Helper, the Holy Spirit, whom the Father will send in My name, He will teach you all things, and bring to your remembrance all things that I said to you." (John 14:25-26, NKJV)

In order for you to successfully crossover from death to eternal life, *at the appointed time*, God has to work his unique miracle. Christ's resurrection demonstrated that He possesses the power to provide you with everlasting life. Death was not eliminated in the resurrection, it was conquered.

This is why the full gospel involves both God's love and power. His love for us would be of little benefit if it ended with our deaths. His love and power are equally important for our eternal assurance.

Therefore, we are informed in Romans 10, the following:

> "But what does it say? *"The word is near you, in your mouth and in your heart"* (that is, the word of faith which we preach): that if you confess with your mouth the Lord Jesus and believe in your heart that God has raised Him from the dead, you will be saved. For with the heart one believes unto righteousness, and with the mouth confession is made unto salvation. For the Scripture says, *"Whoever believes on Him will not be put to shame."* For there is no distinction between Jew and Greek, for the same Lord over all is rich to all who call upon Him. For *"whoever calls on the name of the Lord shall be saved.""* (Romans 10:8-13, NKJV).

These Romans passages sum it up for all who seek to be saved through Christ. We must confess that Jesus Christ is Lord, and believe in our hearts that God raised Him from the dead.

The Sinner's Prayer for Salvation

Knowing that confession of Christ as Lord, coupled with a sincere faith that God raised Him from the dead are salvation requirements, the next step is customarily to recite a sinner's prayer in order to officiate one's salvation.

Definition of the Sinner's Prayer

> *"A sinner's prayer is an evangelical term referring to any prayer of humble repentance spoken or read by individuals who feel convicted of the presence of sin in their life and desire to form or renew a personal relationship with God through his son Jesus Christ. It is not intended as liturgical like a creed or a confiteor. It is intended to be an act of initial conversion to Christianity, and also may be prayed as an act of recommitment for those who are already believers in the faith. The prayer can take on different forms. There is no formula of specific words considered essential, although it usually contains an admission of sin and a petition asking that the Divine (Jesus) enter into the person's life."*[81]

Example of the Sinner's Prayer

Below is a sample Sinner's Prayer taken from the Salvation Prayer website. If you are ready to repent from your sins, and to receive Jesus Christ as your personal Lord and Savior, read this prayer will all sincerity of heart to God.

> Dear God in heaven, I come to you in the name of Jesus. I acknowledge to You that I am a sinner, and I am sorry for my sins and the life that I have lived; I need your forgiveness.

I believe that your only begotten Son Jesus Christ shed His precious blood on the cross at Calvary and died for my sins, and I am now willing to turn from my sin.

You said in Your Holy Word, Romans 10:9 that if we confess the Lord as our God and believe in our hearts that God raised Jesus from the dead, we shall be saved.

Right now I confess Jesus as the Lord of my soul With my heart, I believe that God raised Jesus from the dead. This very moment I receive Jesus Christ as my own personal Savior and according to His Word, right now I am saved.

Thank you Jesus for your unlimited grace which has saved me from my sins. I thank you Jesus that your grace never leads to license for sin, but rather it always leads to repentance. Therefore Lord Jesus transform my life so that I may bring glory and honor to you alone and not to myself.

Thank you Jesus for dying for me and giving me eternal life. Amen.[82]

Congratulations and welcome into the household of God!

Below are the congratulatory words and recommendations also taken from the Salvation Prayer website. If you just prayed the Sinner's Prayer please be sure to read this section for further guidance.

"If you just said this prayer and you meant it with all your heart, we believe that you just got saved and are born again. You may ask, "Now that I am saved, what's next?" First of all you need to get into

a bible-based church, and study God's Word. Once you have found a church home, you will want to become water-baptized. By accepting Christ you are baptized in the spirit, but it is through water-baptism that you show your obedience to the Lord. Water baptism is a symbol of your salvation from the dead. You were dead but now you live, for the Lord Jesus Christ has redeemed you for a price! The price was His death on the cross. May God Bless You!"[83]

Remember, being born again is a spiritual phenomenon. You may have felt an emotional response to your commitment to Christ, but don't be concerned if fireworks didn't spark, bands didn't march, sirens didn't sound, or trumpets didn't blast in the background at the time. There will be plenty of ticker-tape for us in heaven, which is where our rewards will be revealed. If you believed and meant what you said, you can be assured God, Who sent His Son to be crucified on our behalf, heard your every word. Even the angels in heaven are rejoicing.

> *"Likewise, I say to you, there is joy in the presence of the angels of God over one sinner who repents."*(Luke 15:10; emphasis added).

Welcome to the family…!

Endnotes

1   World army rankings taken from the Global Firepower website on July 19, 2018 linked here: https://www.globalfirepower.com/countries-listing.asp

2   The Temple Institutes website is: http://www.templeinstitute.org/

3   List of nations and their relationship to Israel can be found on the Internet as of 5/7/14 at this website: http://en.wikipedia.org/wiki/International_recognition_of_Israel

4   We thank Ned Bankston for researching the headlines concerning the birds of prey gathering in Israel.

5   Reagan quote taken from this weblink: http://christinprophecyblog.org/2017/05/bill-salus-a-true-eschatologist-part-2-of-2/

6   Fruchtenbaum quote came from this website: http://lastdayscalendar.tripod.com/twenty_four_elders.htmThe website quoted from his book called, The Footsteps of the Messiah, p.114

7   Definition of mystery is taken from the New American Standard Exhaustive Concordance.

8   *nikaoô*, translated from the New American Standard Hebrew and Greek Dictionaries

9   Stephanos definition is from Strong's Concordance. It was taken from this website: http://biblehub.com/greek/4735.htm

10   Dr. Reagan book is published by Lamb & Lion Ministries; First edition (October 9, 2012). It is available at his website: www.lamblion.com.

11   Revelation Unveiled by Tim LaHaye page 132.

12   Mark Hitchcock's book called, *The Second Coming of Babylon*, page 161.

13   Wiersbe Expository Outlines on the New Testament – Section: I. The First Seal: Antichrist Rises to Power (6:1-2)

14   The Bible Knowledge Commentary New Testament, by John Walvoord and Roy B. Zuck.

15   John Walvoord article at this weblink: http://walvoord.com/article/264

16   Charles Swindoll's book called, *"Living Insights, New Testament Commentary on the book of Revelation,"* page 113.

17   John Walvoord book entitled, *"Every Prophecy of the Bible,"* on page 606.

18   Tim LaHaye book is entitled, *"Revelation Illustrated and Made Plain,"* page 285.

19   Revelation Unveiled by Tim LaHaye page 271-272

20   Barnes Notes on the New Testament by Albert Barnes… Revelation 17 commentary section.

21   Arno C. Gaebelein, The Revelation, New York, NY, "Our Hope," 1915, pp. 99, 101,102.

22   Pagan Rome and Papal Rome quote taken on 10/6/16 from this website: http://www.reformation.org/pope-constantine.pdf

23   Fish symbol explanation taken from this website: http://www.christianitytoday.com/history/2008/august/what-is-origin-of-christian-fish-symbol.html

24   Foxe's Christian Martyrs of the World, Uhrichsville, OH, Barbour & Company, Inc, pp.64 1990

25   Foxe's Christian Martyrs of the World, Uhrichsville, OH, Barbour & Company, Inc, pp.75-76 1990

26   Zeitoun quote taken from this website: http://www.zeitun-eg.org/zeitoun1.htm

27   Eternal Productions 17 Harvest Road, Fairport, NY 14450. p.5-6

28   Quote taken from the book entitled, "*Queen of All, The Marian apparition's plan to unite all religions under the Roman Catholic Church,*" by Jim Tetlow, Roger Oakland and Brad Myers. Available at Amazon.

29   Petrisko quote taken from his book, "Call of the Ages." Queenship Publishing Santa Barbara, California, 1995, pages 197-198.

30   Isabel Bettwy quote taken from her book called, "I Am The Guardian of the Faith : Reported Apparitions of the Mother of God in Ecuador." The visionary quoted is Patricia (Pachi) Talbot. Franciscan University Press Steubenville, Ohio, 1991, page 63.

31   Consecration defined at this web link: https://www.dictionary.com/browse/consecration

32   Encyclopedia Britannica quote was taken on 9/22/16 from this website link: https://www.britannica.com/place/Seven-Hills-of-Rome

33   J. C. Ryle, Light from Old Times - Volume 1, Charles Nolan Publishers, Moscow, ID, 1890, pages 54-55.

34   The flag of Mohammed is described at this website: http://kenraggio.com/KRPN-GreenHorse.html

35   The flag association between Saudi Arabia and the fourth horseman is made at this website: http://kenraggio.com/KRPN-GreenHorse.html

36   This website also associates Islam with Death and Hades of the fourth seal: http://www.hope-of-israel.org.nz/GreenMustang6.html

37   Quote by Joel Richardson taken from this website on 8/5/18: https://pmicenter.wordpress.com/2013/12/07/muslim-antichrist-explained-by-joel-richardson/

38   Dr. Reagan article available on the web at this link: http://www.lamblion.us/2011/02/muslim-antichrist-theory-joel.html

39   CNN quote taken from this weblink on 8/5/18: https://www.cnn.com/2016/01/26/politics/paul-lepage-maine-guillotine/index.html

40   Quote taken from the web on 8/5/18 at this link: https://www.ibtimes.co.uk/right-wing-french-politician-jean-marie-le-pen-wants-guillotine-reintroduced-terrorists-1529887

41   The Washington Free Beacon article is on the web at this link: https://freebeacon.com/blog/botched-oklahoma-execution-proves-its-time-to-bring-back-the-guillotine/

42   Bring Back the Guillotine article found on the web at this link: http://www.slate.com/articles/news_and_politics/jurisprudence/2013/11/guillotine_death_penalty_lethal_injection_is_cruel_and_unusual_punishment.html

43   Joel Richardson quote from his book called, *Mystery Babylon: Unlocking the Bible's Greatest Prophetic Mystery, page 136.*

44   John Gill quote taken from the internet on 12/15/16 from this website: http://biblehub.com/commentaries/gill/revelation/2.htm

45   Daniel's 70th week is located in Daniel 9:27. This 70th week is also commonly referred to as the Tribulation Period.

46   Dr. David Reagan quote was taken on 12/14/16 from this website: http://christinprophecy.org/articles/the-great-tribulation/

47   Barnhouse quote taken from this website on page 88 of the PDF. http://timothytanministries.yolasite.com/resources/eBook/The%20Invisible%20War%20-%20Donald%20Grey%20Barnhouse%20iPad.pdf

48   Quote taken from the book called, *"A Catechism for Adults,"* page 43.

49   EWTN quote taken from this internet site on 12/15/16: http://www.ewtn.com/library/CATECHSM/NCOFCC.HTM

50   Baltimore Catechisms: Page 256 from this website: https://www.pcpbooks.net/docs/baltimore_catechism.pdf

51   Baltimore Catechisms: Page 290 from this website: https://www.pcpbooks.net/docs/baltimore_catechism.pdf

52   Six days of holy obligation are on Page 292 / #1333 of this website: https://www.pcpbooks.net/docs/baltimore_catechism.pdf

53   Baltimore Catechisms: Page 291 from this website: https://www.pcpbooks.net/docs/baltimore_catechism.pdf

54   Baltimore Catechisms: Page 291 from this website: https://www.pcpbooks. net/docs/baltimore_catechism.pdf

55   Pope John Paul II quote came from this website: http://jimmyakin. com/2010/05/grave-sin-mortal-sin.html

56   Dr. Fruchtenbaum quote taken on 12/7/16 from this website: http://chafer. nextmeta.com/files/v6n1_3.pdf

57   The timing determined to build the third temple is at this website: http:// www.ldolphin.org/gano.html

58   The three prevailing views about the timing of the Third Temple are identified at this website: https://www.breakingisraelnews.com/48944/age-old-biblical-debate-searches-to-answer-which-comes-first-messiah-or-the-temple-jewish-world/#4krHl3HdfclpOBWl.97

59   Ethnos translations taken from the New American Standard Hebrew and Greek Dictionaries under G1484.

60   Pateo translation taken from Strong's Hebrew and Greek Dictionaries under G3961.

61   Plague information was taken on 11/4/16 from this website, http:// ancienthistory.about.com/od/epidemics/tp/10PlaguesEgypt.htm

62   The Revelation Record by Henry M. Morris, Tyndale House Publishers, Inc. Wheaton, Illinois; pages 193-194

63   Jezebel and Harlot parallels were taken from the Queen of All book by Jim Tetlow, Roger Oakland and Brad Myers; pages 112-113

64   Twist of globalisation: All faiths come together article was taken from this website: http://expressindia.indianexpress.com/news/fullstory. php?newsid=35246

65   Quote taken from this website: http://spiralgoddess.com/Mary.html

66   Holman Bible Dictionary under the category of Asherah.

67   Quote taken from Wikipedia at this website: https://en.wikipedia.org/wiki/ Asherah.

68   *Every Prophecy of the Bible*, pages 603 and 612.

69   Verse by Verse Commentary Revelation by John Guzik, page 221.

70   *There's a New World Coming* by Hal Lindsey, page 241.

71   Clarence Larkin, "*The Book of Revelation*," page 153.

72   Tim LaHaye, "Revelation Unveiled," page 277.

73   Web link to Richardson's article: http://www.tedmontgomery.com/ bblovrvw/revelation/MysteryBabylon/01.html

74   God's War on Terror, pages 407-408.

75   Tribulation Road, is the final book of the trilogy and has not been published as of the release of this book.

76   https://www.reuters.com/article/us-saudi-security/iran-aligned-houthis-in-yemen-fire-missiles-at-saudi-capital-idUSKBN1IA100

77   https://www.timesofisrael.com/iran-hails-victory-of-its-proxy-hezbollah-in-lebanon-elections/

78   https://www.reuters.com/article/us-mideast-crisis-syria-israel/israel-strikes-iranian-targets-in-syria-after-rocket-fire-idUSKBN1IA3GF

79   https://www.jpost.com/Middle-East/Hamas-and-Iran-closest-theyve-been-since-Syrian-war-senior-official-says-547353

80   http://www.prophecydepotministries.net/2008/psalm-83-or-ezekiel-38-which-is-the-next-middle-east-news-headline/

81   Sinner's Prayer quote taken from Wikipedia over the Internet on 8/13/11 at this link: http://en.wikipedia.org/wiki/Sinner's_prayer

82   Sinner's prayer example was copied from the Internet on 8/13/11 at this website link: http://www.salvationprayer.info/prayer.html (slight emphasis was added in this appendix)

83   Quote welcoming those who prayed the sinner's prayer into the family of God copied over the Internet on 8/13/11 at this link: http://www.salvationprayer.info/prayer.html

68063431R00133

Made in the USA
Columbia, SC
03 August 2019